CW00740537

JAVA FOR DEVELOPERS

Pocket Primer

JAVA FOR DEVELOPERS
Pocket Primer

Oswald Campesato

MERCURY LEARNING AND INFORMATION
Dulles, Virginia
Boston, Massachusetts
New Delhi

Publisher: David Pallai

Mercury Learning and Information
22841 Quicksilver Drive
Dulles, VA 20166
info@merclearning.com
www.merclearning.com
800-232-0223

O. Campesato. *JAVA for Developers Pocket Primer.*
ISBN: 978-1-68392-549-1

The publisher recognizes and respects all marks used by companies, manufacturers, and developers as a means to distinguish their products. All brand names and product names mentioned in this book are trademarks or service marks of their respective companies. Any omission or misuse (of any kind) of service marks or trademarks, etc. is not an attempt to infringe on the property of others.

Library of Congress Control Number: 2022943450
222324321 This book is printed on acid-free paper in the United States of America.

Our titles are available for adoption, license, or bulk purchase by institutions, corporations, etc. For additional information, please contact the Customer Service Dept. at 800-232-0223(toll free).

All of our titles are available in digital format at *academiccourseware.com* and other digital vendors. Companion files (figures and code listings) for this title are available by contacting info@merclearning.com. The sole obligation of Mercury Learning and Information to the purchaser is to replace the disc, based on defective materials or faulty workmanship, but not based on the operation or functionality of the product.

I'd like to dedicate this book to my parents – may this bring joy and happiness into their lives.

Contents

PREFACE

WHAT IS THE GOAL?

The goal of this book is to provide a reasonably thorough introduction to Java development to people who are relatively new to the Java programming language. The biggest challenge for a book of this length is to provide adequate coverage of some fundamental aspects of Java that are illustrated via code samples that are primarily for Java 8. As this book goes to print, Java 17 is the production release. If you are planning to write a Java application, you need to determine the versions of Java that contain the functionality that you need in your application, after which you can determine the version(s) that you need to install.

WHY THE FOCUS ON JAVA8?

Great question! If you work with modern browsers, you might know about the "browser wars" and also the incompatibility issues that arose in different versions of the same browser (and the relief when the problematic versions were discontinued).

Fortunately, the situation regarding different versions of Java is much more benign (the main source of discontent was the proprietary nature of Java, which eventually led to OpenJDK).

Java 8 was a significant milestone for Java in terms of significant new features, which introduced not only Collections, but also lambda expressions, functional programming, and Streams, all of which are also discussed in this book (along with code samples).

Knowledge of the core features of Java8 will serve you well for subsequent versions of Java. If you are interested, a comprehensive look at Java8 is here:

https://dzone.com/articles/j%CE%BBv%CE%BB-8-a-comprehensive-look

Another useful article that contains many of the new features in Java11 (and details regarding the Long-Term Support for Java8 and Java11) is here:

https://dzone.com/articles/when-will-java-11-replace-java-8-as-the-default-jaTBD

https://www.javacodegeeks.com/2019/11/supporting-java-8.htmlTBD

HOW CAN YOU COVER JAVA IN A 200 PAGE BOOK?

Clearly this book is ambitious, and therefore it's vitally important to articulate a realistic set of expectations. First, you need some object-oriented programming experience, or at least be able to learn OO concepts on your own time (fortunately there are many free online tutorials). Second, consider the fact that there are Java books containing more than 600 pages that do not cover everything about Java.

Hence, this book can only cover a portion of Java. Some Java topics are covered lightly (but often with links where you can find additional information) in order to focus on the key idea. Some Java topics are omitted entirely because they do not belong in a short book about Java.

WHY BUY THIS BOOK IF THERE ARE FREE CODE SAMPLES ONLINE?

The value of this book is the convenience of having a set of illustrative examples in one location, along with all the code samples in the companion files. While free code samples are useful, don't forget that you need to spend time searching for relevant code samples and then spend time reading them. You also need to determine which code samples are up-to-date and actually work correctly (which also takes time). This book saves you this potentially time-consuming process. The question that you need to answer is simple: does the value of your time exceed the cost of this book?

HOW WERE THE CODE SAMPLES CREATED?

The code samples are derived in various ways, such as custom written code (by the author), variations of code from the Java documentation, and sections of code from discussions in online forums.

The code samples attempt to adhere to the "Four Cs": they must be Clear, Concise, Complete, and Correct to the extent that it's possible to do so, given the limitations of the size of this book and the importance of each code sample in relation to the other code samples in this book.

Code samples are available for downloading by writing to the publisher at info@merclearning.com.

WHAT YOU NEED TO KNOW FOR THIS BOOK

You need an understanding of OOP (Object Oriented Programming), Java, and XML. Knowledge of another OO programming language instead of Java might be sufficient, but to be on the safe side, glance through the code samples to gauge whether or not you can manage the material.

THE TARGET AUDIENCE

This book is intended to reach an international audience of developers with highly diverse backgrounds in various age groups. While many readers know how to read English, their native spoken language is not English (which could be their second, third, or even fourth language). Consequently, this book uses standard English and avoids colloquial expressions that might be confusing to those readers. As you know, many people learn by different types of mimicry, which includes reading, writing, or hearing new material. This book takes these points into consideration in order to provide a comfortable and meaningful learning experience for the intended readers.

GETTING THE MOST FROM THIS BOOK

Some developers learn well from prose, others learn well from sample code (and lots of it), which means that there's no single style that works perfectly for everyone.

Moreover, some programmers want to run the code first, see what it does, and then return to the code to understand the details (and others use the opposite approach).

Consequently, there is a variety of code samples in this book. Some are short, some are long, and other code samples "build" from earlier code samples.

HOW DOES THIS BOOK HELP ME?

You will acquire an understanding of various "core" concepts in Java, along with an understanding of how to use many Java APIs. What you decide to learn about Java after you finish reading this Java Primer depends on your goals and career path. For example, if you are a developer, you will undoubtedly continue learning more about Java. On the other hand, if you are in management, you will understand enough about Java to interact on a technical level with Java developers.

WHAT IS THE DEVELOPMENT STACK FOR THE CODE SAMPLES?

The code samples in this book were developed using an early release of Java 13 on a MacBook Pro with OS X 10.10 (Mavericks).

WHY SO MANY SHORT CODE SAMPLES?

This book is for developers who are new to Java development. The code samples are intended to help you gain an understanding of various Java APIs, and that's why every code sample is at most two pages in length (and often less than one page). The focus is to provide code for Java features that you are likely to need in your Java applications. Shorter code samples means that more Java APIs can be included in this book.

HOW WAS THE TABLE OF CONTENTS DETERMINED?

The decision process was as objective as possible, and it involved several criteria. The first criterion was to include "must have" concepts that are common in Java applications. The second criterion was to include "nice to have" functionality that would appeal to Java novices. The third criterion involved Java APIs that could be relevant useful for people who want to write "serious" Java applications.

Examples of such APIs include social connectivity (Facebook and Twitter). The fourth criterion involved Java APIs that are needed for Java applications in the book.

WHICH JAVA TOPICS ARE EXCLUDED AND WHY?

The Java features that do not meet any of the criteria listed in the previous section are not included in this book. Consequently, there is no coverage of Java Native Interface (JNI), which allows Java code to invoke C/C++ functions. In addition, AWT, Java Swing, JavaFX, Java Servlets, JSPs, JAXB, JAXP, JAXR, JEE, and Java Security are not covered in this book. However, you can find a plethora of online blog posts and articles that discuss these topics.

WHAT SHOULD I READ AFTER FINISHING THIS BOOK?

The answer to this question varies widely, mainly because the answer depends heavily on your objectives. Specifically, you need to decide how much effort you are prepared to invest in furthering your knowledge. The amount of time that you need to make significant advances in your technical expertise also depends on your current level of technical knowledge and experience. For instance, the needs of a manager, a student, and a professional Java developer (among others) are obviously different.

With the preceding points in mind, one recommendation involves 1) asking friends and coworkers for advice and suggestions, 2) determining the major features of Java-based projects (either personal or work-related), and 3) performing an Internet search and spend some time evaluating other resources that are available.

CHAPTER 1

INTRODUCTION TO JAVA

This chapter introduces the basic features of Java, along with code samples that illustrate those features. In many cases, the accompanying explanations of the Java code are succinct, especially when the purpose of the purpose of the code is intuitive. The files for this book contain additional code samples that illustrate other features of Java that are not covered in this chapter.

The first part of this chapter contains a very brief introduction to Java, as well as a link for downloading Java onto your machine. You will also learn about Java data types and operators, as well as their precedence.

The second section shows you how to create, compile, and launch a Java class from the command line. You will learn how to create a "Hello World" code sample and how to work with numbers, random numbers, and trigonometric functions in Java.

The third section briefly covers Java characters and strings, and the purpose of the new operator. You will also learn how to determine if two strings are equal, and some other useful string-related function in Java.

Note that occasionally you will see references to a Java class that is not fully explained in the chapter. For example, Listing 1.17 contains an example of autoboxing that invokes the ArrayList class without an explanation of the latter class. However, this happens infrequently, and you can find additional details using online documentation.

One other detail: the last two code samples in this chapter are marked "optional" because you can skip them and proceed directly to Chapter 2 with no loss of continuity. They are included in case you are eager to see code samples that go beyond the basic concepts illustrated in the other code samples in this chapter.

A VERY BRIEF INTRODUCTION TO JAVA

Java is an object-oriented programming language that enables you to run your code on many different hardware platforms, including desktops, mobile devices, and Raspberry PI.

You need to install a platform-specific Java distribution for each platform where you intend to launch Java code (see the next section for details). Although Java 17 is the current production version of Java, earlier versions of Java are still supported.

Java Release Dates

The following bullet list contains the release dates of Java, ranging from Java 7 to Java 18:

- Java SE 7 (July/2011)
- Java SE 8 (March/2014)
- Java SE 9 (Sept/2017)
- Java SE 10 (Mar 2018)
- Java SE 11 (Sept/2018)
- Java SE 12 (March/2019)
- Java SE 13 (Sept/2019)
- Java SE 14 (March/2020)
- Java SE 15 (Sept/2020)
- Java SE 16 (March/2021)
- Java SE 17 (Sept/2021)
- Java SE 18 (July/2022)

As you can see, six years elapsed between Java7 and Java9, after which new Java versions were released at a more accelerated rate.

The following link contains a diagram of the Java 2021 roadmap as well as a layout of Java features:

https://medium.com/javarevisited/the-java-programmer-roadmap-f9db163ef2c2

If you want to learn about the new features that were introduced in different Java releases, visit the following website:

https://www.javatpoint.com/history-of-java

Downloading a Java Release (Short Version)

In view of the many Java releases that are available, how do you decide which version will be best for you? The answer to this question probably involves one or more of the following:

- The version of Java that your company uses
- The latest LTS (long term support)

- The version of Java that you prefer
- The latest version of Java
- The features of Java that you need

One other point to keep in mind: you can also download multiple versions of Java onto your machine if you want to address all the points in the preceding bullet list.

After you have made a determination regarding the version(s) of Java that will work best for you, navigate to the following website and then download the Java distribution for your machine:

https://docs.oracle.com/javase/10/install/toc.htm

SELECTING A VERSION OF JAVA (DETAILED VERSION)

Java 17 is available as this book goes to print, and Java 18 will be released in July 2022. Older versions of Java had release cycles that sometimes involved three or more years, whereas newer versions of Java have been released every six months. The newer releases usually have a much more limited set of updates.

Java 8 and Java 11

Java 8 and Java 11 previously had LTS (Long Term Support) status and currently Java 17 has LTS status. Due to various factors, some large companies are still working with Java 8, which was one of the most significant releases in the history of Java. If you are interested, the Oracle website contains a list of the features of Java 8. In fact, almost all the features in Java 8 will work correctly in all subsequent releases, up to and including Java 17.

However, Java 8 and Java 11 have been deprecated, and currently Java 17 has LTS status. So, which version of Java is recommended? The answer depends on your requirements. If you are unencumbered with maintaining or developing code for older Java versions, then it's probably safe to work with Java 17. If you don't have a choice, then consider working with Java 13, Java 11, or Java 8 (in this order).

Navigate to the following URL for information regarding earlier versions of Java and release dates for future versions of Java:

https://www.oracle.com/java/technologies/java-se-support-roadmap.html

Java Version Numbers

Up until Java 8, the numbering sequence had the form 1.x. Hence, Java 7 was also called Java 1.7, and Java 8 was called Java 8. However, this older naming convention has been dropped starting from Java 9. For example, if you type the command `java -version` and you have `Java` 13 installed on your machine, you will see something similar to the following output:

```
java 13.0.1 2019-10-15
Java(TM) SE Runtime Environment (build 13.0.1+9)
Java HotSpot(TM) 64-Bit Server VM (build 13.0.1+9, mixed
mode, sharing)
```

Aim for a solid grasp of `Java` 13, and then increase your knowledge by learning about the new features that are available in versions after `Java` 13.

JRE Versus a JDK

A JRE (Java Runtime Environment) enables you to launch `Java` code, which means that a Java provides the `java` command-line tool. If you are on a Unix/Linux type of machine, type the following command:

```
$ which java
```

The preceding command displays the following type of output:

```
$ /usr/bin/java
```

On the other hand, a JDK (Java Development Kit) enables you to compile and launch `Java` code. Although the JRE and JDK were available as separate downloads until `Java` 8, they have been merged: i.e., starting from `Java` 9, the Java download is the JDK with the JRE included.

Java Distributions

There are various sites offering the several Java JDKs: the OpenJDK project, the OracleJDK, and AdoptOpenJDK. The OpenJDK Project is the only project site that contains the `Java` source code.

Oracle provides OpenJDK, which is free to use for your Java applications. Updates for older versions are not supported: for example, as soon as `Java` 13 was available, updates to `Java` 12 were discontinued. Oracle also provides OracleJDK, which is free to use only during development: if you deploy your code to a production environment, you must pay a fee to Oracle (which will provide you with additional support).

You can also use AdoptOpenJDK, which was developed by various developers and vendors, and is freely available (just like OpenJDK).

JAVA IDEs

Many people prefer to work in an IDE, and there are very good IDEs available for many programming languages. For example, if you plan to develop Android applications, it's worthwhile to do so in Android Studio, which is an alternative for people who are unfamiliar with the command line.

If you want to write Java code in an IDE (Integrated Development Environment), there are various IDEs that support Java, such as NetBeans and

Eclipse. However, this book focuses on working with `Java` from the command line, and you can create Java classes with a text editor of your choice (or if you prefer, from an IDE). Developing Java code from the command line involves simple manual steps, such as updating the `CLASSPATH` environment variable to include `JAR` files and sometimes also including compiled `Java` class files.

This chapter also contains a brief section that shows you how to create a simple `JAR` file that contains compiled Java code, and after adding this `JAR` file to the `CLASSPATH` variable, you will see how to invoke your custom `Java` code in your custom `JAR` file. Keep in mind that the `Java` code samples in this book are short (and often simple) enough that you don't need an IDE.

JAVA DATA TYPES, OPERATORS, AND THEIR PRECEDENCE

`Java` supports the usual set of primitive types that are available in other compiled languages. In addition, Java provides object-based counterparts. For example, the primitive types `int`, `double`, and `float` have the class-based counterparts `Integer`, `Double`, and `Float`, respectively.

Some data structures, such as hash tables, do not support primitive data types, so the class-based counterparts are necessary. For instance, if you need a hash table to maintain a set of integers, you need to create an `Integer`-based object containing each integer and then add that object to the hash table. Whenever you retrieve a specific `Integer`-based value object from that hash table, you then extract its underlying `int` value. This approach involves slightly more code than simply storing and retrieving `int` values in a hash table. Moreover, `Java` provides eight primitive data types that are keywords in the language:

- byte: 8-bit signed two's complement integer
- short: 16-bit signed two's complement integer
- int: 32-bit signed two's complement integer
- long: 64-bit signed two's complement integer
- float: single-precision 32-bit IEEE 754 floating point
- boolean: either true or false
- char: single 16-bit Unicode character

Most of the code samples in this book that involve arithmetic calculations use integers and floating point numbers.

Java Comments

`Java` supports one-line comments as well as multi-line comments, both of which are shown here:

```
// this is a one-line comment
/* this is a multi-line comment that uses a C-style syntax
// and can include the one-line comment style
*/
```

However, `Java` does not support nested comments (and neither does C/C++), so this is an error:

```
/* first comment /* start of second comment */ end of first
*/
```

Based on the earlier examples, the following syntax *is* correct for a comment:

```
/* first comment // start of second comment end of first */
```

Java Operators

`Java` supports the usual set of arithmetic operators, along with the standard precedence (exponentiation has higher priority than multiplication * and division /, both of which have higher priority than addition + and subtraction - . In addition, Java supports the following operators:

- Arithmetic operators: +, -, °, /, %, ++, and --
- Assignment operators: =, +=, -=, °=, /=, %=, <<=, >>=, &=, ^=, and !=
- Bitwise Operators: &, |, ^, and ~
- Boolean operations: `and`, `or`, `not`, and `xor`
- Logical Operators: &&, ||, and !
- Relational operators: ==, !=, >, <, >=, and <=

`Java` also supports the ternary operator ? and the operator `instanceOf` that checks if a variable is an instance of a particular class.

Precedence of Java Operators

Operator precedence determines the grouping of terms in an expression, which in turn determines how an expression is evaluated. Higher precedence operators are evaluated before lower precedence operators, even when they appear inside expressions.

Java operators are listed below, from highest to lowest precedence (LTR means left-to-right and RTL means right-to-left):

```
• LTR Postfix:            () [] . (dot operator)
• RTL Unary:              ++ - - ! ~
• LTR Multiplicative:     * / %
• LTR Additive:           + -
• LTR Shift:              >> >>> <<
• LTR Relational:         > >= < <=
• LTR Equality:           == !=
• LTR Bitwise AND:        &
• LTR Bitwise XOR:        ^
• LTR Bitwise OR:         |
• LTR Logical AND:        &&
• LTR Logical OR:         ||
```

- RTL Conditional: ?:
- RTL Assignment: = += -= *= /= %= >>= <<= &= ^= |=
- LTR Comma: ,

For example, x is assigned the value 20 instead of 36 in the following expression because * has higher precedence than +:

```
x = 8+4*3;
```

If necessary, use parentheses to change the order of the evaluation of an expression:

```
y = (5+4)*3;
```

The value of y in the preceding code snippet is 27.

The += operator is a shorthand way of incrementing a value, and both of the following code snippets are equivalent:

```
x = x + 5;
x += 5;
```

The -= operator is a shorthand way of decrementing a value, and both of the following code snippets are equivalent:

```
x = x - 5;
x -= 5;
```

The ++ operator is a shorthand way of incrementing a value, and the following code snippets perform the same arithmetic computation:

```
x += 1;
x++;
++x;
```

However, there is an important difference: the ++ operator is performed *first* if it appears on the left-side of a variable, and it's performed *second* if it appears on the right side of a variable. Consider this code snippet:

```
x = 3;
if( x++ == 3) { x = 7; }
```

The if statement in the preceding code snippet is true because the logical comparison is performed before incrementing x. Here's the question: will x equal 4 or will it equal 7 after the if statement? (Answer: 7).

Consider this code snippet in which the ++ appears on the *left-side* of the variable x:

```
x = 3;
if( ++x == 3) { x = 7; }
```

The if statement in the preceding code snippet is false because the ++ operator first increments the value of x from 3 to 4, after which the comparison is false. Hence, the value of x is *not* updated from 4 to 7 (i.e., it's still 4). If you are comfortable with Java classes, you can compile and launch the code sample `DoubleOperator.java` that contains the preceding code snippets.

Similar comments apply to the – operator: the left-side occurrence of – is performed first, whereas the right-side occurrence is performed second.

Java also supports multiple initializations of variables. For example, consider the following code snippet:

```
int a, b, c, d;
a = b = c = d = 77;
```

After the preceding assignments are executed, all four variables have the value 77.

Note that a floating point variable that is initialized as an integer value will "promote" the integer to a decimal value. Consider the following code block:

```
int a = 5;
float f;
f = a;
float g = a;
```

After the assignments are executed, the output will be as follows:

```
a: 5
f: 5.0
g: 5.0
```

The opposite conversion will not work, as shown here:

```
// possible lossy conversion error:
//int b = g;

// this assignment is correct.
int c = (int)g;
```

The value of c after the preceding initialization is 5 (not 5.0). See the Java class `IntAndFloat.java` for the complete code sample.

CREATING AND COMPILING JAVA CLASSES

Let's start with the simplest possible Java class that does nothing other than display the basic structure of a Java class. Listing 1.1 displays the contents of `MyClass.java` that defines the Java class `MyClass`.

LISTING 1.1: MyClass.java

```
public class MyClass
{
}
```

The first point to notice is that the name of the file in Listing 1.1 is the same as the Java class `MyClass` that is qualified by the keywords `public` and class. You can have more than one class in a `Java` file but only one of them can be public, and that public class in the file must match the name of the file.

Open a command shell, navigate to the directory that contains `MyClass.java`, and compile `MyClass.java` from the command line with the `javac` executable:

```
javac MyClass.java
```

The `javac` executable creates a file called `MyClass.class` that contains `Java` bytecode. Launch the Java bytecode with the Java executable (do not include any extension):

```
java MyClass
```

Note that you do not specify the suffix `.java` or `.class` when you launch the `Java` bytecode. The output from the preceding command is here:

```
Exception in thread "main" java.lang.NoSuchMethodError: main
```

Note: The name of a file with `Java` source code must match the public `Java` class in that file. For example, the file `MyClass.java` must define a `Java` class called `MyClass`.

We can fix the previous error in Listing 1.2, which contains a `main` method that serves as the initial "entry point" for launching a `Java` class from the command line.

LISTING 1.2: MyClass.java

```
public class MyClass
{
    // this code does nothing
    public static void main(String[] args){}
}
```

Listing 1.2 contains the `public static method main()`, whose return type is `void` because it returns nothing. The `main()` method is `static`, which ensures that it will be available when we launch the `Java` class from the command line. Now compile the code again:

```
javac MyClass.java
```

Launch the class from the command line:

```
java MyClass
```

You have now successfully created, compiled, and launched a `Java` class called `MyClass` that still does nothing other than compile successfully. The next step involves displaying a text string in a `Java` class, which is discussed in the next section.

A "HELLO WORLD" EXAMPLE

Listing 1.3 displays the contents of `HelloWorld1.java` that shows you how to print the string "Hello World" from a `Java` class.

LISTING 1.3: HelloWorld1.java

```java
public class HelloWorld1
{
    public static void main (String args[])
    {
        System.out.println("Hello World");
    }
}
```

The code in Listing 1.3 shows a routine called `main()` that contains a `System.out.println()` statement that prints the string "Hello World." Open a command shell to compile and launch the `Java` code in Listing 1.3:

```
javac HelloWorld1.java
```

Launch the compiled code by typing the following command:

```
java HelloWorld1
```

The output from the preceding command is here:

```
Hello World
```

Now that you see how easy it is to create and compile a simple `Java` program, let's look at examples of working with numbers in `Java`.

WORKING WITH NUMBERS

Listing 1.4 displays the content of `Numbers.java` that shows you how to work with integers and decimal values. In this code sample, we're glossing over the details of Java strings, but they will be discussed in more detail later in this chapter.

LISTING 1.4: Numbers.java

```java
public class Numbers
{
    public static void main (String args[])
    {
        // int and double are primitive types:
        int x1 = 3, x2 = 7;
        System.out.println("x1: "+x1+" x2: "+x2);

        // Integer and Double are class types:
        Integer a1 = 3, a2 = 5;
        Double  b1 = 3.2, b2 = 5.7;
        System.out.println("a1: "+a1+" a2: "+a2);
        System.out.println("b1: "+b1+" b2: "+b2);
```

```
String s1 = "3", s2 = "5";
String t1 = a1.toString();
String t2 = Integer.toString(a1);

System.out.println("s1: "+s1);
System.out.println("s2: "+s2);
System.out.println("t1: "+t1);
System.out.println("t2: "+t2);
System.out.println("t1 == s1: "+(t1 == s1));
System.out.println("t2 == s1: "+(t2 == s1));

double y1=5.2, y2=-3.6;
double w1 = Math.ceil(y1);
double w2 = Math.ceil(y2);

System.out.println("y1: "+y1);
System.out.println("y2: "+y2);
System.out.println("w1: "+w1);
System.out.println("w2: "+w2);
  }
}
```

Listing 1.4 defines the Java class Numbers and a main() method that contains familiar arithmetic calculations. As an early preview, Listing 1.4 contains the Integer class, which is a "wrapper" around the primitive type int. The Integer class has some useful methods, such as Integer.toString() that converts an integer value to its string-based counterpart.

Note the use of the Math.ceil() method to find the ceiling of a number. Launch the compiled code by typing the following command:

```
java Numbers
```

The output from the preceding command is here:

```
x1: 3 x2: 7
a1: 3 a2: 5
b1: 3.2 b2: 5.7
s1: 3
s2: 5
t1: 3
t2: 3
t1 == s1: false
t2 == s1: false
y1: 5.2
y2: -3.6
w1: 6.0
w2: -3.0
```

Working with Other Bases

Although numbers in Java are base 10 by default, Java also supports binary, octal, and hexadecimal. Hexadecimal numbers start with 0x or 0X, as shown here:

```
int hex = 0xFF;
```

Octal values start with 0, as shown here:

```
int oct = 011;
```

WORKING WITH RANDOM NUMBERS

Listing 1.5 displays the content of RandomNumbers.java that shows you how to work with random numbers in Java. Although this code sample contains a loop that we will discuss in greater detail in Chapter 2, the code in Listing 1.5 is straightforward and easy to understand.

LISTING 1.5: RandomNumbers.java

```
public class RandomNumbers
{
    public static void main (String args[])
    {
        int die1, die2, sum, maxValue=6, loopCount=10;

        for(int i=0; i<loopCount; i++)
        {
            die1 = (int)(maxValue*Math.random()) + 1;
            die2 = (int)(maxValue*Math.random()) + 1;
            sum = die1 + die2;

            System.out.println("die1: "+die1+" die2: "+die2+"
            sum "+sum);
        }
    }
}
```

Listing 1.5 defines the Java class RandomNumbers and a main() method with a loop that executes 10 times (the value of loopCount), from 0 through 9. During each iteration, the code in the loop initializes the integer valued-variables die1 and die2 as randomly generated numbers via the Math.random() method, as shown here:

```
die1 = (int)(maxValue*Math.random()) + 1;
die2 = (int)(maxValue*Math.random()) + 1;
```

The method Math.random() returns a decimal value (such as 3.187), so we need to cast the return value with (int), as shown in bold in the preceding code snippet. The minimum possible value is 0, so we need to add 1 to the right-hand side of die1 and die2 so that the minimum value is 1. Since maxValue is 6, the maximum value for die1 and die2 is 6, and therefore their sum will be an integer between 2 and 12, inclusive. Launch the code in Listing 1.5 and you will see the following output:

```
die1: 3 die2: 1 sum 4
die1: 6 die2: 6 sum 12
die1: 3 die2: 6 sum 9
die1: 2 die2: 4 sum 6
```

```
die1: 6 die2: 4 sum 10
die1: 4 die2: 6 sum 10
die1: 5 die2: 2 sum 7
die1: 1 die2: 3 sum 4
die1: 2 die2: 1 sum 3
die1: 4 die2: 5 sum 9
```

WORKING WITH BUILT-IN MATH FUNCTIONS

Java supports many useful mathematical functions. Listing 1.6 displays the content of MathFunctions.java that shows you how to invoke various mathematical functions.

LISTING 1.6: MathFunctions.java

```java
public class MathFunctions
{
    public static void main (String args[])
    {
        double a = 7, b = 3;

        // the square root of b:
        System.out.println("Square root of b: " + Math.sqrt(b));

        // a raised to the power of b:
        System.out.println("Power of a and b is: "+Math.pow(a,b));

        // the logarithm of a and b:
        System.out.println("Logarithm of a: " + Math.log(a));
        System.out.println("Logarithm of b: " + Math.log(b));

        // Euler's e (~2.17828...) raised to the power a:
        System.out.println("Exponential of a: " +Math.exp(a));

        // the minimum and maximum of two numbers
        System.out.println("Minimum of a and b: "+Math.min(a,b));
        System.out.println("Maximum of a and b: "+Math.max(a,b));
    }
}
```

Listing 1.6 shows you how to calculate square roots, exponential values, and logarithms of numbers, as well as the minimum and maximum of a pair of numbers. Launch the code in Listing 1.6 and you will see the following output:

```
Square root of b: 1.7320508075688772
Power of a and b is: 343.0
Logarithm of a: 1.9459101490553132
Logarithm of b: 1.0986122886681098
Exponential of a: 1096.6331584284585
Minimum of a and b: 3.0
Maximum of a and b: 7.0
```

WORKING WITH BUILT-IN TRIGONOMETRIC FUNCTIONS

Listing 1.7 displays the content of `TrigFunctions.java` that shows you how to perform various operations on numbers that involve trigonometric functions.

LISTING 1.7: TrigFunctions.java

```
public class TrigFunctions
{
    public static void main (String args[])
    {
        // default is degrees:
        double a = 45;

        // degrees to radians (pi/4):
        double b = Math.toRadians(a);

        // sine, cosine, and tangent of a:
        System.out.println("Sine of a: " +Math.sin(a));
        System.out.println("Cosine of a: " +Math.cos(a));
        System.out.println("Tangent of a: " +Math.tan(a));

        // arc sine and hyperbolic sine of a:
        System.out.println("Arc Sine of a: " +Math.asin(a));
        System.out.println("Hyperbolic Sine of a: "+Math.
        sinh(a));
    }
}
```

Listing 1.7 starts by initializing the variable a with the value 45 and then initializes the variable b with the radian-based value of a. The next portion of Listing 1.7 calculates the sine, cosine, and tangent values of the variable a. The final portion of Listing 1.7 calculates the arc sine and hyperbolic sine of the variable a. Launch the code in Listing 1.7 and you will see the following output:

```
Sine of a: 0.8509035245341184
Cosine of a: 0.5253219888177297
Tangent of a: 1.6197751905438615
Arc Sine of a: NaN
Hyperbolic Sine of a: 1.7467135528742547E19
```

WORKING WITH BITWISE OPERATORS

This section shows you how to perform bit-wise operations on numbers, using logical operators such as OR ("^"), AND ("&"), and NOT ("~"). Listing 1.8 displays the content of `Bitwise.java` that shows you how to perform various bitwise operations on two integers.

LISTING 1.8: Bitwise.java

```java
public class Bitwise
{
    // Bitwise Operators: &, |, ^, and ~
    // XOR (^) function:
    // 0 ^ 0 = 0
    // 0 ^ 1 = 1
    // 1 ^ 0 = 1
    // 1 ^ 1 = 0

    public static void main(String[] args)
    {
        int num1, num2;

        num1 = 5;      // Binary: 00101
        num2 = 10;     // Binary: 01010

        System.out.println("num1:     " + num1);
        System.out.println("num2:     " + num2);
        System.out.println("~num1:    " + (~num1));
        System.out.println("num1^num2: " + (num1^num2));
        System.out.println("num1&num2: " + (num1&num2));
        System.out.println("num1|num2: " + (num1|num2));
        System.out.println("");

        num1 = 16;     // Binary: 010000
        num2 = 32;     // Binary: 100000

        System.out.println("num1:     " + num1);
        System.out.println("num2:     " + num2);
        System.out.println("~num1:    " + (~num1));
        System.out.println("num1^num2: " + (num1^num2));
        System.out.println("num1&num2: " + (num1&num2));
        System.out.println("num1|num2: " + (num1|num2));
    }
}
```

Listing 1.8 initializes the variables num1 and num2, and then performs various bit-related operations, such as inverting the value of num1 and then calculating the XOR, AND, and OR values of num1 and num2. Launch the code in Listing 1.8 and you will see the following output:

```
num1:      5
num2:      10
~num1:     -6
num1^num2: 15
num1&num2: 0
num1|num2: 15

num1:      16
num2:      32
~num1:     -17
num1^num2: 48
num1&num2: 0
num1|num2: 48
```

THE JAVA STRING CLASS

A variable of type `char` is a single character that you can define via the `char` keyword like this:

```
char ch1 = 'Z';
```

A variable of type `String` is an object that comprises a sequence of character values. Java also supports ASCII, UTF8, and Unicode characters. The `java.lang.String` class implements the interfaces `Serializable`, `Comparable`, and `CharSequence`.

If you are familiar with interfaces, then the following sentences in this paragraph will make sense. The `Serializable` interface does not contain methods: it's essentially a "marker" interface, whereas the `CharSequence` interface is for sequences of characters. In addition to the Java `String` class, the `StringBuffer` class and the `StringBuilder` class implement the `CharSequence` interface (more details later). If you are unfamiliar with interfaces, you will learn about them in Chapter 4, after which you can re-read this paragraph.

Keep in mind the following point: every Java `String` is immutable, and to modify a string (such as append or delete characters), Java creates a *new* instance "under the hood" for us. Yes, this means that string-related operations are less memory efficient; however, Java provides the `StringBuffer` and `StringBuilder` classes for mutable Java strings (also discussed later).

An array of characters is effectively the same as a Java `String`:

```
char[] chars = {'h','e','l','l','o'};
String str1  = new String(chars);
String str2  = "hello";
```

You can access a character in a string with the `charAt()` method, as shown here:

```
char ch = str1.charAt(1);
```

The preceding code snippet assigns the letter "e" to the character variable `ch`. You can assign a single quote mark to `ch2` with this code snippet:

```
char ch2 = '\'';
```

Characters, Arrays, and Strings in Java

Listing 1.9 displays the contents of `CharsStrings.java` that shows you how to define characters, arrays, and strings.

LISTING 1.9: CharsStrings.java

```
public class CharsStrings
{
    public CharsStrings(){}
```

```java
public static void main (String args[])
{
    char ch1 = 'Z';
    char ch2 = '\'';

    char[] chars = {'h','e','l','l','o'};
    String str1  = new String(chars);
    String str2  = "hello";
    String str3  = new String(chars);
    String str4  = Character.toString(ch2);

    System.out.println("ch1:    "+ch1);
    System.out.println("ch2:    "+ch2);
    System.out.println("chars: "+chars);

    System.out.println("str1:   "+str1);
    System.out.println("str2:   "+str2);
    System.out.println("str3:   "+str3);
    System.out.println("str4:   "+str4);
}
}
```

Listing 1.9 initializes the variables ch1 and ch2 as single characters, followed by the variable chars as a sequence of characters. The variables str1 through str4 are initialized in various ways as string-based variables. Launch the code in Listing 1.9 and you will see the following output:

```
ch1:    Z
ch2:    '
chars: [C@5451c3a8
str1:  hello
str2:  hello
str3:  hello
str4:  '
```

The output of the chars variable might be different from what you expected. You can use a loop to display the characters in the chars variable. Here's a simple example of a loop (compare this syntax with the earlier loop) that displays the content of the chars variable:

```java
System.out.print("chars: ");
for(char ch : chars)
{
    System.out.print(ch);
}
System.out.println();
```

The output from the preceding loop is here:

```
chars: hello
```

Java Strings with Metacharacters

Java treats metacharacters in a string variable in the same manner as any other alphanumeric character. Thus, you don't need to "escape" metacharacters in Java strings, whereas it's necessary to do so when you define a `char` variable (see the `ch2` variable in the preceding code sample).

You can concatenate two `Java` strings by "adding" them together, as shown here:

```
String first = "John";
String last  = "Smith";
String full  = first + " " + last;
```

Java treats the following code snippet in a slightly different way:

```
String first = "John";
String last  = "Smith";
first = first + " " + last;
```

The variables `first` and `last` are initialized with string values, and then a new block of memory is allocated that is large enough to hold the contents of the variable `first`, the blank space, and the contents of the variable `last`. These three quantities are copied into the new block of memory, which is then referenced by the variable `first`.

As you might have already surmised, many large string-related operations can be time-consuming and memory-intensive. Fortunately, there is a more efficient alternative that's discussed in Chapter 3. Listing 1.10 displays the content of `Strings.java` that initializes and then prints several strings.

LISTING 1.10: MyStrings.java

```
public class Strings
{
   public static void main (String args[])
   {
      String str1 = "John", str2 = "Sally";
      String str3 = "*?)",   str4 = "+.@";
      String str5 = "\n\n", str6 = "\t";

      System.out.println("str1: "+str1+" str2: "+str2);
      System.out.println("str3: "+str3+" str4: "+str4);
      System.out.println("str5: "+str5+" str6: "+str6);
   }
}
```

Listing 1.10 defines the `Java` class `MyStrings` and a `main()` method that initializes the strings `str1` through `str6` with names, metacharacters, and whitespaces. The three `println()` statements display their values, as shown here:

```
str1: John str2: Sally
str3: *?) str4: +.@
str5:

 str6:
```

There is no visible difference between a space and a `tab` character in the preceding output, but you *can* see the difference in the `vi` editor. First, redirect the output of the preceding code to a file called `out1` (or some other convenient name). Next, open the file in the `vi` editor, and then type `:set list`, after which you will see the following output:

```
str1: John str2: Sally$
str1: John str2: Sally$
str3: *?) str4: +.@$
str5: $
$
 str6: ^I$
```

The `$` indicates the end of a line, which appears at the end of every line in the preceding output. Notice that the last line displays `^I$`, which indicates the presence of the `tab` character that is the value of the `str6` variable in Listing 1.10.

THE JAVA NEW OPERATOR

The previous section contains several examples of directly assigning a string in `Java`. Another way to do so involves the `new` operator, which superficially looks the same, but it has an important distinction. When you initialize two variables with the same string, in the manner shown in Listing 1.11, they occupy the same memory location. When you use the `new` operator, the two variables will occupy different memory locations.

Listing 1.11 displays the content of `ShowPeople.java` that uses the `new` operator to initialize two strings and then print their values.

LISTING 1.11: ShowPeople.java

```java
public class ShowPeople
{
    // cannot be initialized in main()
    String str5, str6;

    public ShowPeople(){}

    public static void main (String args[])
    {
        String str1, str2, str3, str4;

        // str1 and str2 occupy different memory locations
        str1 = new String("My name is John Smith");
        str2 = new String("My name is John Smith");

        // str3 and str4 occupy the same memory location
        str3 = "My name is Jane Andrews";
        str4 = "My name is Jane Andrews";

        System.out.println(str1);
        System.out.println(str2);
```

```
        System.out.println(str3);
        System.out.println(str4);

        // error: non-static variable str5 cannot
        // be referenced from a static context:
      //str5 = new String("another string");
      //str6 = new String("yet another string");
      }
   }
```

Listing 1.11 contains a `main()` routine that defines and initializes the string variables `str1` through `str4` and then prints their contents. The output from Listing 1.11 is here:

```
My name is John Smith
My name is John Smith
My name is Jane Andrews
My name is Jane Andrews
```

The code in Listing 1.11 contains hard-coded values and therefore has no reusability. For example, suppose that you want to print all the names that are defined in arrays containing the names `people`. Perhaps you want to print names that are randomly selected from those arrays. You might even want to get a person's first name and last name from the command line and then print the person's name.

The next section provides more details regarding the difference between "==" and the `equals()` method in the Java `String` class.

EQUALITY OF STRINGS

Unlike other languages, the "==" operator does not determine whether two strings are identical: this operator only determines if two variables are referencing the same *memory* location. The `equals()` method compares the *content* of two strings whereas the == operator matches the *object* or reference of the strings.

Listing 1.12 displays the content of `EqualStrings.java` that illustrates how to compare two strings and determine if they have the same value or the same reference (or both).

LISTING 1.12: EqualStrings.java

```
import java.io.IOException;

public class EqualStrings
{
    public static void main(String[] args) throws
IOException
    {
        String str1 = "Pizza";
        String str2 = "Pizza";
```

```
    if (str1.equals(str2))
    {
        System.out.println("str1 and str2: equal values");
    }

    if (str1 == str2)
    {
        System.out.println("str1 and str2: equal
        references");
    }
    System.out.println("");

    String str3 = "Pasta";
    String str4 = new String("Pasta");

    if (str3.equals(str4))
    {
        System.out.println("str3 and str4: equal values");
    }
    else
    {
        System.out.println("str3 and str4: unequal values");
    }

    if (str3 == str4)
    {
        System.out.println("str3 and str4: equal
references");
    }
    else
    {
        System.out.println("str3 and str4: unequal
references");
    }
  }
}
```

Listing 1.12 defines the Java class EqualStrings and a main() method that defines the string variables str1, str2, str3, and str4. Launch the code in Listing 1.12 and you will see the following output:

```
str1 and str2: equal values
str1 and str2: equal references

str3 and str4: equal values
str3 and str4: unequal references
```

When you create a string literal, the JVM (Java Virtual Machine) checks for the presence of that string in something called the "string constant pool." If that string exists in the pool, then Java simply returns a reference to the pooled instance; otherwise, a new string instance is created (and it's also placed in the pool).

The next section contains a Java code sample that illustrates how to determine whether two strings are identical.

Comparing Strings

Listing 1.13 displays the content of CompareStrings.java that illustrates how to compare two strings and determine if they have the same value or the same reference (or both).

LISTING 1.13: CompareStrings.java

```
public class CompareStrings
{
    public CompareStrings(){}
    public static void main (String args[])
    {
        String line1 = "This is a simple sentence.";
        String line2 = "this is a simple sentence.";

        System.out.println("line1: "+line1);
        System.out.println("line2: "+line2);
        System.out.println("");

        if (line1.equalsIgnoreCase(line2)) {
            System.out.println(
                "line1 and line2 are case-insensitive equal");
        } else {
            System.out.println(
                "line1 and line2 are case-insensitive
                different");
        }

        if (line1.toLowerCase().equals(line1)) {
            System.out.println("line1 is all lowercase");
        } else {
            System.out.println("line1 is mixed case");
        }
    }
}
```

Listing 1.13 defines the Java class CompareStrings and a main() method that defines the string variables line1 and line2. Launch the code in Listing 1.13 and you will see the following output:

```
line1: This is a simple sentence.
line2: this is a simple sentence.

line1 and line2 are case-insensitive same
line1 is mixed case
```

SEARCHING FOR A SUBSTRING IN JAVA

Listing 1.14 displays the content of SearchString.java that illustrates how to use the indexOf() method to determine whether a string is a substring of another string. Note that this code sample involves an if statement, which is discussed in more detail in the final code sample of this chapter.

LISTING 1.14: SearchString.java

```
public class SearchString
{
    public SearchString(){}
    public static void main (String args[])
    {
        int index;
        String str1 = "zz", str2 = "Pizza";

        index = str2.indexOf(str1);
        if(index < 0)
        {
            System.out.println(str1+" is not a substring of
            "+str2);
        }
        else
        {
            System.out.println(str1+" is a substring of
            "+str2);
        }
    }
}
```

Listing 1.14 contains the `main()` method that calculates the index of the string `str1` in string `str2`, which has the value 2. Launch the code in Listing 1.14 and you will see the following output:

```
zz is a substring of Pizza
```

USEFUL STRING METHODS IN JAVA

The Java `String` class supports a plethora of useful and intuitively-named methods for string-related operations, including `compare()`, `compareTo()`, `concat()`, `equals()`, `intern()`, `length()`, `replace()`, `split()`, and `substring()`.

The `String` class has some very useful methods for managing strings, some of which are listed here (and one of which you have seen already):

- substring(idx1, idx2): the substring from index idx1 to idx2
- compareTo(str): compare a string to a given string
- indexOfStr(str): find the index of a string in another string
- lastIndexOfStr(str): find the index of the last occurrence of a string in another string

Listing 1.15 displays the content of `CapitalizeFirstAll.java` that illustrates how to use the `substring()` method to capitalize the first letter of each word in a string, how to convert the string to all lowercase letters, and how to convert the string to all uppercase letters. Note that this example uses a loop.

LISTING 1.15: CapitalizeFirstAll.java

```java
public class CapitalizeFirstAll
{
   public CapitalizeFirstAll(){}

   public static void main (String args[])
   {
      String line1 = "this is a SIMPLE sentence.";
      String[] words = line1.split(" ");
      String line2 = "", first = "";
      for(String word: words)
      {
         first = word.substring(0,1).toUpperCase()+word.
         substring(1);
         line2 = line2 + first + " ";
      }

      System.out.println("line1: "+line1);
      System.out.println("line2: "+line2);

      String upper = line1.toUpperCase();
      String lower = line1.toLowerCase();

      System.out.println("Lower: "+lower);
      System.out.println("Upper: "+upper);
   }
}
```

Listing 1.15 defines the Java class `CapitalizeFirstAll` and a `main()` method that initializes the `String` variable `line1` with a text string. The next portion of the `main()` method splits ("tokenizes") the contents of `line1` into an array of words via the `split()` method.

Next, a loop iterates through each word in the `words` array, and sets the variable `first` equal to the uppercase version of the first letter of the current word, concatenated with the remaining letters of the current word, as shown here:

```java
first = word.substring(0,1).toUpperCase()+word.
substring(1);
```

The final portion of the `main()` method displays the contents of the modified sentence, along with a lowercase version of the sentence, followed by an uppercase version of the original sentence. Launch the code in Listing 1.15 and you will see the following output:

```
line1: this is a SIMPLE sentence.
line2: This Is A SIMPLE Sentence.
Lower: this is a simple sentence.
Upper: THIS IS A SIMPLE SENTENCE.
```

Parsing Strings in Java

Java supports command-line arguments, which enables you to launch programs from the command line with different command line values. Compare two `Java` strings with the `equals()` method to determine whether the values are the same. Although some languages compare strings via "==", in Java, the "==" only compares the two references (not the values) of two strings.

Use the `parseInt()` method to (attempt to) convert a string to an integer:

```
int num = Integer.parseInt("1234");
```

Use the `substring()` method to split a string with white space characters:

```
String[] strArray = aString.split("\\s+");
```

The regular expression `\s+` matches one or more occurrences of various white space characters, including " ", "\t", "\r", and "\n".

A very simple way to reverse a `Java` string is with this code snippet:

```
String rev = new StringBuilder(original).reverse().
toString();
```

Thus far, you have seen various examples of working with strings in `Java`, and for more information, navigate to this URL:

https://docs.oracle.com/javase/7/docs/api/java/lang/String.html

OVERRIDING THE JAVA TOSTRING() METHOD (OPTIONAL)

You have already seen several examples of the `toString()` method in existing Java classes, such as `Integer.toString()` and `Character.toString()`.

The `toString()` method of the `Object` class, which is the parent of all classes in `Java`, returns a string representation of any object in `Java`. The default `toString()` method of the `Object` class displays a combination of the object class and its hash code as a mechanism by which you can distinguish between different instances of the same Java class. An example of the output of the default `toString()` method is shown here:

```
OverrideToString@4dc63996
```

However, it's possible to override the `toString()` method to return something else for the string representation of your custom class.

Listing 1.16 displays the content of `OverrideToString.java` that illustrates how to override the `toString()` method that belongs to the `Object` class in order to return a new string representation for the custom Java class.

LISTING 1.16: *OverrideToString.java*

```
public class OverrideToString
{
    private String fname = "John";
    private String lname = "Smith";

    public OverrideToString(){}
```

```
public String toString()
{
    return fname + " " + lname;
}

public static void main (String args[])
{
    OverrideToString ots = new OverrideToString();
    System.out.println("Overriding toString(): "+ots.
    toString());
}
}
```

Listing 1.16 contains the variables fname, lname, and the toString() method that concatenates the values of fname and lname. Launch the code in Listing 1.16 and you will see the following output:

```
Overriding toString(): John Smith
```

Incidentally, if you "comment out" the toString() method in Listing 1.16, you will see the following output from the default toString() method:

```
OverrideToString@4dc63996
```

AUTOBOXING AND UNBOXING (OPTIONAL)

The term *autoboxing* is the automatic conversion that the Java compiler makes between the primitive types and their corresponding object wrapper classes. For example, autoboxing converts an int to an Integer, a double to a Double, and so on. The term *unboxing* refers to the situation in which the conversion is performed in the opposite direction.

Autoboxing and unboxing enables you to write cleaner code, which in turn makes it easier to read your code. The following table lists the *primitive* types and their corresponding wrapper classes, which are used by the Java compiler for autoboxing and unboxing:

```
boolean Boolean
byte    Byte
char    Character
float   Float
int     Integer
long    Long
short   Short
double  Double
```

Here is the simplest example of autoboxing:

```
Character ch = 'a';
```

The remaining examples in this section use generics. If you are not yet familiar with the syntax of generics, there are online articles available with detailed explanations.

Consider the following code that involves the `ArrayList` class and a `for` loop that appends 50 numbers to the variable `items`:

```
List<Integer> items = new ArrayList<>();
for (int i = 1; i < 50; i += 2)
    items.add(i);
```

Although you add the `int` values as primitive types instead of `Integer` objects to the variable items, the code compiles correctly. Since `items` is a list of `Integer` objects, not a list of `int` values, you may wonder why the Java compiler does not issue a compile-time error. The compiler does not generate an error because it creates an `Integer` object from `i` and adds the object to `items`. Thus, the compiler converts the previous code to the following at runtime:

```
List<Integer> items = new ArrayList<>();
for (int i = 1; i < 50; i += 2)
    items.add(Integer.valueOf(i));
```

As another example of auto boxing, consider the following method:

```
public static int sumEven(List<Integer> items)
{
    int sum = 0;

    for (Integer i: items)
        if (i % 2 == 0)
            sum += i;

        return sum;
}
```

Since the remainder (`%`) and unary plus (`+=`) operators do not apply to `Integer` objects, why does the Java compiler successfully compile the preceding method? The reason is that the compiler invokes the `intValue()` method to convert an `Integer` to an `int` at runtime:

```
public static int sumEven(List<Integer> li)
{
    int sum = 0;
    for (Integer i : li)
        if (i.intValue() % 2 == 0)
            sum += i.intValue();
        return sum;
}
```

Listing 1.17 displays the content of `Unboxing.java`, which is a complete code sample of autoboxing in Java.

LISTING 1.17: _Unboxing.java_

```
import java.util.ArrayList;
import java.util.List;
```

```
public class Unboxing
{
    public static void main(String[] args)
    {
        Integer i = new Integer(-8);

        // 1) Unboxing through method invocation
        int absVal = absoluteValue(i);
        System.out.println("absolute value of "+i+" =
        "+absVal);

        List<Double> ld = new ArrayList<>();
        ld.add(3.1416); // π is autoboxed through method
        invocation

        // 2) Unboxing through assignment
        double phi = ld.get(0);
        System.out.println("phi = "+phi);
    }

    public static int absoluteValue(int i)
    {
        return (i < 0) ? -i : i;
    }
}
```

Launch the code in Listing 1.17 and you will see the following output:

```
absolute value of -8 = 8
phi = 3.1416
```

SUMMARY

This chapter introduced you to some Java features, such as some of its supported data types, operators, and the precedence of Java operators. You also learned how to instantiate objects that are instances of Java classes, and how to perform arithmetic operations in a main() method.

Then you saw how to work with numbers, random numbers, and trigono-metric functions in Java. In addition, you received an overview of characters and strings, and the significance of the new operator. Finally, you learned how to determine if two strings are equal, and some other useful string-related functions in Java.

CHAPTER 2

BOOLEAN LOGIC, UNICODE, USER INPUT

This chapter introduces you to various topics in Java: how to use conditionals, how to work with dates, examples of Unicode, and how to handle user input. You will also learn how to use try/catch code blocks whenever you try to convert a string to a numeric value.

The first section discusses conditional logic, with if-then statements, and nested if-then statements in a Java code sample that determines whether a positive integer is a leap year. The second section shows you how to work with dates in Java, along with a code sample that involves Unicode strings for Japanese and Mandarin.

The third part of this chapter shows you how to prompt users for input and how to use try/catch blocks to handle exceptions that can arise while attempting to convert input strings to numbers or decimal values. You will also see an example of a try/catch/finally code block in a Java class to handle exceptions.

CONDITIONAL LOGIC IN JAVA

Conditional logic enables you to make decisions based on logical conditions. The simplest type of conditional logic involves an "if" statement, and when additional conditional statements are required, you can use if-else statements and if-else-if statements.

Another Java construct is the switch statement, which also involves conditional logic: you can experiment with both techniques to determine which tasks are better suited to a switch statement instead of multiple if-else statements.

As a starting point, Listing 2.1 displays the content of Conditional1.java that performs modulo arithmetic and uses the integer-valued remainder to print various messages.

LISTING 2.1: Conditional1.java

```java
public class Conditional1
{
    int x = 12, y = 15;
    public Conditional1() {}
    public void IfElseLogic()
    {
        if(x % 2 == 0) {
            System.out.println("x is even: "+x);
        } else if(x % 4 == 0) {
            System.out.println("x is divisible by 4: "+x);
        } else {
            System.out.println("x is odd: "+x);
        }

        if(x % 2 == 0) {
            if(x % 4 == 0) {
                System.out.println("x is divisible by 4: "+x);
            }
        }

        if(y % 3 == 0 && y % 5 == 0) {
            System.out.println("y is divisible by 3 and 5: "+y);
        } else if(y % 3 == 0) {
            System.out.println("y is divisible only by 3: "+y);
        } else if(y % 5 == 0) {
            System.out.println("y is divisible only by 5: "+y);
        } else {
            System.out.println("y is not divisible by 3 or 5: "+y);
        }
    }

    public static void main(String args[])
    {
        Conditional1 c1 = new Conditional1();
        c1.IfElseLogic();
    }
}
```

Listing 2.1 defines the Java class Conditional1 and the public method IfElseLogic() that performs modulo arithmetic on the integer variables x and y that are initialized with the values of 12 and 15, respectively.

If x % 2 equals 0, then x is even; if x % 4 equals 0, then x is a multiple of 4; if y % 3 equals 0, then y is a multiple of 3. Listing 2.1 contains if-else code blocks, one of which is a nested block of conditional logic. Try to determine the output of the code block that you can compare with the generated output. Now launch the code in Listing 2.1 and you will see the following output:

```
x is even: 12
x is divisible by 4: 12
y is divisible by 3 and 5: 15
```

You can easily create much more complex Boolean expressions involving multiple combinations of "and," "or," and "not" (this involves "!="). Use the code in Listing 2.1 as a baseline from which you can add your own variations.

The next section shows you how to work with Boolean expressions involving numbers and strings in Java.

WORKING WITH BOOLEAN EXPRESSIONS

This section shows you how to create Boolean expressions based on a comparison of various scalar types. Listing 2.2 displays the content of `BooleanExamples.java` that compares integers, doubles, and characters.

Although most of the results will be what you expect, there might be some surprises: see how many values you can predict correctly and then compare your answers with the output.

LISTING 2.2: BooleanExamples.java

```
public class BooleanExamples
{
    public static void main(String[] args)
    {
        // working with integers and double (floating point)
        int int1 = 5;
        double double1 = 3.53;
        double double2 = 54.88;

        System.out.println("int1 = " + int1);
        System.out.println("double1 = " + double1);
        System.out.println("double2 = " + double2);
        System.out.println("");

        System.out.println("int1 < 5: " + (int1 < 5));
        System.out.println("double1 > double2: "+(double1 >
        double2));
        System.out.println("");

        // int1 and integer 3 promoted
        System.out.println("int1 >= double1: "+ (int1
        >=double1));
        System.out.println("double1 <= 3: " + (double1 < 3));
        System.out.println("");

        // working with characters
        char char1 = 'A';
        char char2 = 'C';

        System.out.println("char1 = " + char1);
        System.out.println("char2 = " + char2);
        // lexicographical comparison
        System.out.println("char1 < char2: " + (char1 <
        char2));

        // A:65, B:66, C:67, ..., Z:90
        // a:97, b:98, c:99, ..., z:122
        // char2 promoted to decimal value (67)
```

```
    System.out.println("10 > char2: " + (10 > char1));
    System.out.println("");

    boolean mixed = (int1 == 5) || char1 < 'A' && double1
    != 21.8;
    System.out.println("mixed: " + mixed);
    System.out.println("");

    // working with boolean values

    boolean bool1 = false;
    boolean bool2 = true;

    System.out.println("bool1: " + bool1);
    System.out.println("bool2: " + bool2);
    System.out.println("bool1 == bool2: " + (bool1 ==
    bool2));
    System.out.println("bool1 =  bool2: " + (bool1 =
    bool2));
    System.out.println("");

    String str1 = new String("Pizza1");
    String str2 = new String("Pizza2");
    System.out.println("str1: " + str1);
    System.out.println("str2: " + str2);

    // compare contents of str1 and str2
    System.out.println("str1 == str2: " + (str1 == str2));
    System.out.println("str1 = str2: " + (str1 = str2));
  }
}
```

Listing 2.2 contains various Java data types, including integers, floating point values, character values, and Boolean values. Launch the code in Listing 2.2 and you will see the following output:

```
int1 = 5
double1 = 3.53
double2 = 54.88

int1 < 5: false
double1 > double2: false

int1 >= double1: true
double1 <= 3: false

char1 = A
char2 = C
char1 < char2: true
10 > char2: false

mixed: true

bool1: false
bool2: true
bool1 == bool2: false
bool1 =  bool2: true

str1: Pizza1
str2: Pizza2
str1 == str2: false
str1 = str2: Pizza2
```

Notice the output shown in bold: the first section displays `true`, even though `bool1` was assigned the value `false`. This happened because the "=" operator is an assignment operator: consequently, hence `bool1` is assigned the value of `bool2`, with the result that the new value of `bool1` is `true`.

In a similar fashion, the second output that's shown in bold displays the string `Pizza2` because the "=" operator assigned the value of `str2` (which is `Pizza2`) to the string `str1`.

WORKING WITH DATES

The `Java` package `java.util` contains the `Date` class that encapsulates the current date and time. The `Date` class supports an empty constructor that initializes the object with the current date and time. The second constructor accepts one argument that equals the number of milliseconds that have elapsed since midnight, January 1, 1970:

```
Date(long millisec).
```

The Current Date and Time

Listing 2.3 displays the content of `DateTime.java` that illustrates how to use a `Date` object with the `toString()` method to print the current date and time.

LISTING 2.3: DateTime.java

```java
import java.util.Date;
public class DateDemo
{
    public static void main(String args[])
    {
        // instantiate a Date object
        Date date = new Date();

        // display time and date using toString()
        System.out.println(date.toString());
    }
}
```

Compile and launch the code in Listing 2.3 and you will see the following output:

```
Fri Aug 13 09:51:52 CDT 2021
```

Date Comparison

`Java` also provides several methods for calendar dates, some of which are shown below:

- `getTime()` returns the number of milliseconds that have elapsed since midnight, January 1, 1970
- the methods `before()`, `after()`, and `equals()`

As a simple example, the 12th of any month obviously precedes the 18th of any month, and so new Date(99, 2, 12).before(new Date (99, 2, 18)) returns true.

Date Formatting with SimpleDateFormat

The SimpleDateFormat class is a concrete class for formatting and parsing dates in a locale-sensitive manner. SimpleDateFormat allows you to start by choosing any user-defined patterns for date-time formatting.

Listing 2.4 displays the content of SimpleDate1.java that illustrates how to use a SimpleDateFormat object with the toString() method to print the current date and time.

LISTING 2.4: SimpleDate1.java

```java
import java.util.*;
import java.text.*;

public class SimpleDate1
{
   public static void main(String args[])
   {
      Date dNow = new Date();
      SimpleDateFormat ft =
         new SimpleDateFormat("E yyyy.MM.dd 'at' hh:mm:ss a
         zzz");

      System.out.println("Current Date: " +
      ft.format(dNow));
   }
}
```

Compile and launch the code in Listing 2.4 and you will see the following output:

```
Fri Aug 13 09:51:52 CDT 2021
```

Parsing Strings as Dates

The SimpleDateFormat class contains the parse() method for parsing a string based to the format stored in the given SimpleDateFormat object.

Listing 2.5 displays the content of StringToDate1.java that illustrates how to use a StringToDate1 object with the toString() method to print the current date and time.

LISTING 2.5: StringToDate1.java

```java
import java.util.*;
import java.text.*;

public class StringToDate1
{
   public static void main(String args[])
```

```
    {
        SimpleDateFormat ft = new SimpleDateFormat ("yyyy-MM-
        dd");

        // notice the ternary operator here:
        String input = args.length == 0 ? "1818-11-11" :
        args[0];
        System.out.print(input + " Parses as ");
        Date t;

        try {
            t = ft.parse(input);
            System.out.println(t);
        } catch (ParseException e) {
            System.out.println("Unparseable using " + ft);
        }
    }
}
```

Listing 2.5 defines the `Java` class `StringToDate1` and a `main()` method that defines the variable `ft` as an instance of the `SimpleDate` class. The `input` variable is initialized via the ternary operator "?", which will be initialized with the string `"1818-11-11"` if no command-line arguments are specified; otherwise, the `input` variable is assigned the value of `args[0]`, which is the first (left-most) command line argument.

The next portion of the `main()` method contains a `try/catch` block to convert `input` to a valid date: if the value of `input` is an invalid date format, the `catch()` code block is executed and a suitable message is displayed. Now compile and launch the code in Listing 2.5 and you will see the following output:

```
Thu Aug 13 09:51:52 CDT 2021
```

The `java.time` package (packages are discussed later) also contains other useful classes, some of which are given here:

```
LocalDate
LocalTimeLocalDateTime
Period
Duration
```

If you need to work with dates in `Java` code, perform an online search for detailed explanations and Java code samples.

WORKING WITH UNICODE, i18n, AND i10n

This section briefly discusses `UTF-8` and `Unicode` support in `Java`, along with a code sample that displays text written in Mandarin and in Hiragana (phonetic Japanese lettering).

The `Unicode` Standard provides a unique number for every character in every written language. Moreover, `Unicode` is supported on major operating systems, search engines, browser, laptops, and smart phones.

As of May 2019, Unicode 12.1 contains 137,994 characters covering 150 modern and historic scripts, along with multiple symbol sets and emoji. Unicode can be implemented by different character encodings, including UTF-8, UTF-16, and UTF-32 (and several other encodings), but they do not provide full support for Unicode.

Java supports UTF-8, which is the dominant encoding on the Web (used in over 94% of websites). UTF-8 uses one byte for the first 128 code points, and up to 4 bytes for other characters. The first 128 Unicode code points represent the ASCII characters, which means that any ASCII text is also UTF-8 text. See the following Wikipedia page for more information about Unicode:

https://en.wikipedia.org/wiki/Unicode

In addition, navigate to the official Unicode website for more information about Unicode:

https://home.unicode.org/

Listing 2.6 displays the content of Unicode.java that contains some code snippets for Unicode.

LISTING 2.6: *Unicode.java*

```
public class Unicode
{
    public Unicode(){}

    public static void main (String args[])
    {
        String mand =
            new String("\u5c07\u63a2\u8a0e DL \u53ca\u5176\
u4ed6");

        String hira =
new String("DL \u306F \u304B\u3063\u3053\u3043\u3043 \
u3067\u3059!");

        System.out.println("Mandarin: "+mand);
        System.out.println("Hiragana: "+hira);
    }
}
```

Listing 2.6 initializes the string variables mand and hira with Unicode characters for Mandarin and Hiragana, respectively. Launch the code and you will see the following output ("DL is cool") in Mandarin and Hiragana:

```
Mandarin: 將探討 DL 及其他
Hiragana: DL は かっこいい です!
```

Although i18n and i10n are similar (and often confused for each other), the main difference is as follows: i18n pertains to displaying text on a Web page in different languages, and `i10n` pertains to "localization," which refers to the display of dates, numbers, and currency in a given language on a Web page.

The implementation of `i18n` involves a file with word/value pairs, with one file for each language. `Java` uses the `Bundle` class and an algorithm to determine which language and region to select, both of which are already assigned on each user's laptop or desktop. For example, a file that contains American English and Italian could contain something like this:

```
hello: ciao
goodbye:ciao
friend: amico
```

Keep in mind that unlike English, words in romance languages (including Italian) and Germanic languages have a gender: Italian has masculine and feminine, whereas German has masculine, feminine, and neuter. Thus, the word *amico* refers to a male friend, whereas *amica* refers to a female friend. Incidentally, some languages (such as Japanese) have no gender.

A highly detailed article that discusses `i18n` and `i10n` is available online:

https://dzone.com/articles/a-beginners-guide-to-java-internationalization

The last topic in this section is `i10n`, which is simpler to illustrate in a code sample involving number formats. Specifically, Listing 2.7 displays the content of `I10NNumberFormats.java` that illustrates the number formats for involving the decimal point and the "thousands" separator for three different languages: English, Italian, and Mandarin.

LISTING 2.7: I10NNumberFormats.java

```java
public class I10NNumberFormats
{
    import java.util.Locale;
    import java.text.NumberFormat;

    public I10NNumberFormats(){}

    public static void main (String args[])
    {
        double d = 123456.789;

        NumberFormat nf1 = NumberFormat.getInstance(Locale.US);
        NumberFormat nf2 = NumberFormat.getInstance(Locale.ITALY);
        NumberFormat nf3 = NumberFormat.getInstance(Locale.CHINA);

        System.out.println("US format of     " +
                        d + ": " + nf1.format(d));

        System.out.println("ITALY format of " +
                        d + ": " + nf2.format(d));
```

```
System.out.println("CHINA format of " +
                    d + ": " + nf3.format(d));
    }
}
```

Listing 2.7 starts with two `import` statements, followed by a `main()` method that contains three instances of the `NumberFormat` class with the three locales (US, Italy, and China). Launch the code and you will see the following output:

```
US format of    123456.789: 123,456.789
ITALY format of 123456.789: 123.456,789
CHINA format of 123456.789: 123,456.789
```

WORKING WITH BASE64

Listing 2.8 displays the content of `Base64Encode.java` that illustrates how to convert a text string into a `base64` encoding and also decode that string into its original format.

LISTING 2.8: Base64Encode.java

```
import java.util.Base64;

public class Base64Encode
{
    public Base64Encode(){}

    public static void main (String args[])
    {
        String original = "New York Pizza";
        String encoded   =
            Base64.getEncoder().encodeToString(original.
            getBytes());

        byte[] decodedBytes  = Base64.getDecoder().
        decode(encoded);
        String decodedString = new String(decodedBytes);

        System.out.println("Original: "+original);
        System.out.println("Encoded:  "+encoded);
        System.out.println("Decoded:  "+decodedString);
    }
}
```

Listing 2.8 defines the class `Base64Encode` and a `main()` method that initializes the string `original` and then converts the text string to its equivalent encoding in `base64`. The next portion of Listing 2.8 reverses the encoding, and then prints the original string, the encoded string, and then the decoded string. Launch the code and you will see the following output:

```
Original: New York Pizza
Encoded:  TmV3IFlvcmsgUGl6emE=
Decoded:  New York Pizza
```

WORKING WITH EXCEPTIONS IN JAVA

An exception occurs when your code expects data of a certain type but data of an incompatible type is received, so your code cannot process that data. Handling exceptions is important because they can occur in various situations, such as an array index that is out of bounds, opening or closing streams, and missing files.

For example, suppose that your code prompts users for numeric input from the command line in order to print twice the input value. If the input string can be converted to a numeric value (such as 123), then your code will work as expected, but if the input string cannot be converted to a numeric value (such as A123), then your code will throw an exception.

Java provides exceptions that handle a variety of scenarios that can occur during the execution of your Java program, some of which are listed here:

- Division by zero exception
- Conversion error (string -> int) exception
- Database exception
- File not found exception
- JVM out-of-memory exception
- Network-related exception

A partial list of so-called "checked" Java exceptions is as follows:

- `ArithmeticException`
- `ClassNotFoundException`
- `InputMismatchException`
- `InvocationTargetException`
- `IOException`
- `NumberFormatException`
- `SQLClientInfoException`
- `SQLException`

The first two exceptions in the preceding list occur during a division by zero (or square root of a negative number) and when a Java class is not found, respectively. The `InputMismatchException` occurs when the token received by a `Scanner` instance does not match the expected type. The `InvocationTargetException` "wraps" an exception that is thrown by an invoked method or a constructor.

An `IOException` occurs during file I/O stream operations (e.g., file not found). A `NumberFormatException` occurs during a conversion between data types (e.g., from a `String` to an `int`). Finally, the two `SQL`-related exceptions pertain to database errors.

For your convenience, the `import` statements for some of the earlier Java exceptions are shown here:

- `import java.io.IOException;`
- `import java.lang.ArithmeticException;`
- `import java.lang.NumberFormatException;`
- `import java.lang.ArrayIndexOutOfBoundsException;`
- `import java.net.MalformedURLException;`
- `import java.util.InputMismatchException;`
- `import java.util.InputMismatchException;`

The Java code samples later in this chapter contain examples of most of the preceding exceptions (i.e., the SQL-related exceptions are not discussed in this book).

Java provides two types of exceptions: checked exceptions and unchecked exceptions, both of which are discussed in the following sections.

Checked Exceptions

Checked exceptions (also called compile-time exceptions) are checked by the compiler during compilation: doing so will confirm whether the exception is handled by the programmer. If not, the system displays a compilation error. For example, SQLException, IOException, InvocationTargetException, and ClassNotFoundException are checked exceptions.

Unchecked Exceptions

Unchecked exceptions (also called Runtime exceptions) in Java occur during the execution of a Java program. In general, runtime exceptions are ignored during the compilation process. They are not checked while compiling the program. Examples include incorrect APIs and logical errors. Unchecked exceptions in Java include the following:

- `ArrayIndexOutofBound`
- `NullPointerException`
- `IllegalArgumentException`
- `IllegalStateException`

An `ArrayIndexOutofBound` exception occurs when your code attempts to access an array element that does not exist: i.e., the index value is invalid (too large or negative).

A `NullPointerException` occurs when your code attempts to access an object that has not been initialized.

An `IllegalArgumentException` occurs whenever the wrong type of argument is passed to a method. For example, if a method expects a variable of type int and you pass a variable of an incompatible type, or you pass a null variable, you will see this exception.

An `IllegalStateException` occurs when the state of the environment does not match the operation being executed.

The throws Keyword

The `throws` keyword indicates the type of exception that a method can throw if the specified exception occurs in the method, in which case the following can occur:

- the calling method handles the thrown exception, or
- its "parent" handles the exception, or
- the "parent" passes the exception upward through the chain of calling methods.

If the exception is not handled by any method in the chain of calling methods, an exception is thrown and the program halts execution.

Alternatively, you can include your code in a `try/catch/finally` block, and the `catch` block specifies the exception that is caught. You can include multiple `catch` blocks, each of which catches a particular exception: the first `catch` block is the most specific (such as `DivisionByZero`), and the last `catch` block is the most "generic" (such as `Exception`).

The Throwable Class

The `Throwable` class is the superclass of all exceptions and errors. Keep in mind the following rule: do not catch a `Throwable` exception in a `catch` clause because it will catch all errors as well as all exceptions. Errors are thrown by the JVM to indicate serious problems (applications are not intended to handle them). Typical examples include the `OutOfMemoryError` or the `StackOverflowError`. Both are caused by situations that are outside of the control of the application and cannot be handled.

One more recommendation: avoid catching an exception and then throwing the same exception again. Doing so generates multiple error message for the same exception.

GETTING USER INPUT AND HANDLING EXCEPTIONS

The code samples involving user input contain a `try` block that attempts to do something, such as converting a string to a number. However, if users provide a non-numeric input, then the conversion will fail, in which case a `catch` block will catch the error that occurred, and the code that appears in the `catch` block is executed.

Moreover, you can include a `finally` block after the `catch` blocks (yes, multiple `catch` blocks are allowed) that is executed in almost every case (the "exception" to this rule pertains to invoking the `System.exit()` statement). Note that if you specify a `try/catch` block in a class when no exception can be thrown, `Java` will alert you during an attempt to compile your code.

The code samples show you two things that have not been discussed yet. First, you will see how to use the `import` statement to access existing classes that handle the lower-level details for us, so we do not need to "reinvent the wheel". Java import statements are tremendously powerful, and almost all the code samples in this book use them.

Second, you will learn how to use try/catch blocks to handle exceptions that can occur when you attempt to convert an input string to an integer or float value. System.in.read() treats the input string as an ASCII value, which means that an input string of 0 is converted to 48, 1 is converted to 49, and so forth.

Listing 2.9 displays the content of UserInput.java that prompts users for a string and then attempts to convert that string to a number. This is the simplest example in this section, and there is no try/catch code block for handling any exceptions.

LISTING 2.9: UserInput.java

```
import java.util.Scanner;

public class UserInput
{
    public static void main (String args[])
    {
        System.out.print("Enter a number: ");
        Scanner scan = new Scanner(System.in);
        int num1 = scan.nextInt();
        System.out.println("you entered a number");
    }
}
```

Listing 2.9 prompts users for their input, which is processed by the variable scan that is an instance of the Scanner class. The nextInt() method of the Scanner class converts the input to an integer value, which is assigned to the variable num1, and then printed via a System.out.println() statement. Here is the output when you launch the code:

```
Enter a number: 123
you entered a number
```

Here is the output when you enter a non-numeric string:

```
Enter a number: x123
Exception in thread "main" java.util.InputMismatchException
    at java.util.Scanner.throwFor(Scanner.java:840)
    at java.util.Scanner.next(Scanner.java:1461)
    at java.util.Scanner.nextInt(Scanner.java:2091)
    at java.util.Scanner.nextInt(Scanner.java:2050)
    at UserInput.main(UserInput.java:9)
```

As you can see, the preceding stack trace is displayed on the command line because this exception is not caught in the code in Listing 2.9.

Let's examine Listing 2.10, which displays the content of UserInput2.java that also prompts users for a string. Notice that this code sample contains is a try/catch block that attempts to convert an input string to a number.

LISTING 2.10: UserInput2.java

```
import java.util.InputMismatchException;
import java.util.Scanner;

public class UserInput2
{
    public static void main (String args[])
    {
        System.out.print("Enter a number: ");
        Scanner scan = new Scanner(System.in);

        try {
            int num1 = scan.nextInt();
            System.out.println(num1+" is a number");
        }
        catch (InputMismatchException ime) {
            System.out.println("You did not enter a number");
            System.out.println("===> Before the stack
            trace...");
            ime.printStackTrace();
            System.out.println("===> After the stack
            trace...");
        }
    }
}
```

Listing 2.10 contains a `try/catch` code block in which the `try` block contains the input-related code, and the `catch` block contains code that is invoked when an error occurs. In particular, we know that an error will occur when users enter a string that cannot be converted to a number. Here is the output when you launch the code:

```
Enter a number: 123
123 is a number
```

Here is the output when you enter a non-numeric string:

```
Enter a number: x123
You did not enter a number
===> Before the stack trace...
java.util.InputMismatchException
    at java.util.Scanner.throwFor(Scanner.java:840)
    at java.util.Scanner.next(Scanner.java:1461)
    at java.util.Scanner.nextInt(Scanner.java:2091)
    at java.util.Scanner.nextInt(Scanner.java:2050)
    at UserInput2.main(UserInput2.java:12)
===> After the stack trace...
```

The code in Listing 2.10 correctly handles the situation when a non-numeric string is entered as an input string. However, in this situation, we do not have the input value because the conversion to num1 (which is of type int) failed. The solution involves capturing the user input as a string, as shown in the next section.

PARSING USER INPUT AND HANDLING EXCEPTIONS

The `Integer` class contains two methods for parsing a string (i.e., converting a string to a number):

```
static int parseInt(String s)
static int parseInt(String s, int radix)
```

The first method (shown in Listing 2.11) uses a default base of 10, whereas the second method allows you to specify a different base. For example, if you want to convert user input to a hexadecimal value, you would specify a radix value of 16.

Listing 2.11 displays the content of `UserInput3.java` that prompts users for a string and then attempts to convert that string to a number. It also captures the user's input string.

LISTING 2.11: UserInput3.java

```java
import java.io.Console;
import java.lang.NumberFormatException;

public class UserInput3
{
   public static void main (String args[])
   {
      Console input = System.console();
      String str1 = input.readLine("Enter a number: ");

      try {
         int num1 = Integer.parseInt(str1);
         System.out.println(str1+" is a number");
      }
      catch (NumberFormatException nfe) {
         System.out.println(str1+" is not a number");
      }
   }
}
```

Listing 2.11 first initializes the variable `input` as an instance of the `Console` class. Next, the string variable `str1` is assigned the value of a user's input, which is "captured" by the `readLine()` method.

At this point, we have the contents of the user's input, and we can use a `try/catch` block to determine whether the input string can be converted to a number. Here is the output when you launch the code:

```
Enter a number: 123
123 is a number
```

Here is the output when you enter a non-numeric string:

```
Enter a number: x123
x123 is not a number
```

The code in Listing 2.11 correctly handles the situation when a non-numeric string is entered as an input string. Notice that there is no stack trace, and we can easily see when the conversion to an integer value fails. Moreover, we can also handle the case when an input string is a floating point number.

Listing 2.12 displays the content of UserInput4.java that prompts users for a string and then attempts to convert that string to an integer. If this fails, the code attempts to convert the string to a decimal number; if this also fails, an error message is displayed.

LISTING 2.12: *UserInput4.java*

```
import java.io.Console;
import java.lang.NumberFormatException;

public class UserInput4
{
    public static void main (String args[])
    {
        Console input = System.console();
        String str1 = input.readLine("Enter a number: ");

        try {
            int num1 = Integer.parseInt(str1);
            System.out.println(str1+" is a number");
        }
        catch (NumberFormatException nfe) {
            System.out.println(str1+" is not an integer ");

            try {
                float dec1 = Float.parseFloat(str1);
                System.out.println(dec1+" is a decimal value");
            }
            catch (NumberFormatException nfe2) {
                System.out.println(str1+" is not a decimal");
            }
        }
    }
}
```

Listing 2.12 contains code that is the same as Listing 2.11, with one difference: the try/catch block contains a second try/catch block that attempts to convert the user's input to a floating point number. Thus, there are two attempts at converting the input string, after which the code determines that the input is a non-numeric string. Here is the output when you launch the code:

```
Enter a number: 123.4
123.4 is not an integer
123.4 is a decimal value
```

Here is the output when you enter a non-numeric string:

```
Enter a number: x123
x123 is not an integer
x123 is not a decimal
```

This concludes the basic introduction to user input and how to use a try/catch block to handle conversion errors.

NESTED EXCEPTIONS

Java provides a number of classes for handling exceptions that can occur in various situations. For example, when you attempt to open a file that does not exist, Java throws a FileNotFoundException. If you attempt to convert a string containing alphabetic characters to a number, you get an exception. If you try to access a table that does not exist in a database, you will also get an exception.

The general syntax is try/catch/finally, which can involve multiple catch statements. If an exception is thrown, each catch block is checked to see if it matches the exception. If the thrown exception does not match any of the specified exceptions, you can include a "catch all" exception that is invoked when nothing else matches the exception.

Another point to keep in mind is that the finally code block is optional; however, when it's specified in your code, that code block is always guaranteed to execute, regardless of whether any errors occurred.

Listing 2.13 displays the content of the class ConvertString1.java that illustrates how to use the valueOf() and parseInt() methods to convert an Integer and an int, respectively.

LISTING 2.13: ConvertString1.java

```java
import java.lang.NumberFormatException;

public class ConvertString1
{
    public ConvertString1() {}

    public void convert(String str)
    {
        Integer x;
        int y;

        System.out.println("String: "+str);

        try {
            x = Integer.valueOf(str);
            y = Integer.parseInt(str);

            System.out.println("x:      "+x);
            System.out.println("y:      "+y);
            System.out.println();
        }
        catch(NumberFormatException nfe) {
            System.out.println("Cannot convert "+str+" to an
            int");
        }
    }
}
```

```
public static void main(String args[])
{
    String str1 = "123";
    String str2 = "456a";

    ConvertString1 cs1 = new ConvertString1();
    cs1.convert(str1);
    cs1.convert(str2);
}
}
```

Listing 2.13 has rearranged the code in Listing 2.12 by placing the try/
catch block in the convert() method that takes a parameter of type String
and attempts to convert the parameter to an integer.

The code style for Listing 2.13 is sort of a prelude to the object-oriented
style of code that you can write in Java. We'll look at this code style in more
detail in Chapter 3, which introduces you to accessors, mutators, and over-
loaded constructors.

Notice that the main() method creates an instance cs1 of the
ConvertString1 class, after which the convert() method can be invoked
because it's defined in the class ConvertString1. In fact, the convert()
method is invoked twice: the first time with the variable str1 (which can be
converted to an integer) and the second time with the variable str2 (which
cannot be converted to an integer). Launch the code in Listing 2.13 and you
will see the following output:

```
String: 123
x:      123
y:      123
String: 456a
Cannot convert 456a to an int
```

A TRY/CATCH/FINALLY EXAMPLE

Listing 2.14 displays the content of the class DivideByZero.java that
illustrates how to prompt for user input, and then convert that input to a
numeric value in a try/catch/finally code block. Notice that a second try/
catch/finally code block handles the division-by-zero case.

```
Listing 2.14: DivideByZero.java
import java.lang.ArithmeticException;
import java.util.InputMismatchException;
import java.util.Scanner;

public class DivideByZero
{
    public static void main (String args[])
    {
        int numer = 3, denom = 0;
        double ratio = 0.0;

        System.out.print("Enter a number: ");
        Scanner scan = new Scanner(System.in);
```

```
try {
    denom = scan.nextInt();
    System.out.println(denom+" is a number");

    try {
        ratio = (double)numer/denom;
        System.out.println("1ratio = "+ratio);
    }
    catch (ArithmeticException ae) {
        System.out.println("=> 1Cannot divide by
        zero");
    }
    finally {
        System.out.println("first finally block");
    }
}
catch (InputMismatchException ime) {
    System.out.println("You did not enter a number");
    System.out.println("Trying to divide by zero");

    try {
        ratio = (double)numer/denom;
        System.out.println("2ratio = "+ratio);
    }
    catch (ArithmeticException ae) {
        System.out.println("=> 2Cannot divide by
        zero");
    }
    finally {
        System.out.println("second finally block");
    }
}
}
}
```

Listing 2.14 defines the class `DivideByZero` and a `main()` method that contains a `try/catch` block. The `try` block itself contains a `try/catch/finally` block that prompts users for input, and attempts to convert the input to a numeric value.

If the conversion is successful, the code computes the ratio of `numer` and `denom`, where the latter is the numeric value of the input. If the denominator is 0, then the `catch` block displays a message that division by zero is not allowed; otherwise, the ratio of `numer`/`denom` is displayed.

If the conversion to a numeric value is *not* successful, the top-level `catch` code block is executed, which displayed a suitable message, and then the `finally` block is executed.

SUMMARY

This chapter introduced you to conditional logic with if-then statements and nested if-then statements to perform multiple conditional logic. Next you learned how to work with the `Date` class, and how you can convert a string to a date with a specified format.

You also learned how to work with `Unicode`, along with an example involving text strings in Japanese and Mandarin. You then got a brief introduction to `i18n` and `l10n` for internationalization and localization.

Then you saw how to obtain user input and how to use `try/catch` blocks and `try/catch/finally` blocks while attempting to convert strings to numbers and to decimal values.

CHAPTER 3

METHODS AND CONSTRUCTORS

This chapter describes different types of methods that you can define in a custom Java class. You will also learn about the different permission levels to invoke methods and access variables in a Java class. In addition, this chapter contains code samples that illustrate about various ways to invoke Java constructors and methods.

The first part introduces you to the public, protected, and private attributes for methods, as well as variables in a Java class, and how these attribute determine the accessibility of variables and methods in a given Java class from other Java classes.

The second part of this chapter discusses static variables, static methods, and static code blocks in a Java class. Next, you will learn how to construct arrays of instances of a custom Java class.

The third part of this chapter contains five Java code samples to illustrate various ways that you can invoke a constructor in a custom Java class. This section also introduces you to anonymous inner classes, Java named inner classes, and private constructors.

The fourth part of this chapter discusses the Java import statement and explains the purpose of the package statement, along with some code samples that show you how to use the package statement.

The final portion of this chapter discusses JAR files, as well as their purpose and how to use the jar utility to create JAR files.

WHAT IS A JAVA CLASS?

As you have seen in previous code samples, a Java class consists of methods and data, and an object is an instance of a Java class. An object is created via the new keyword. The filename and the name of the class inside the file must be the same. For example, the file `MyClass.java` must contain a public class called `MyClass`. A Java class can contain other Java classes, but they are private classes. Java also supports the concept of anonymous inner classes, which are often used for the implementation of event listeners of GUI widgets.

A class can only subclass a *single* class via the `extends` keyword; hence, Java does not support the multiple inheritance of classes. However, a class can implement multiple interfaces via the `implements` keyword. An *abstract* class contains at least one method that must be implemented by a subclass. Thus, abstract classes cannot be directly instantiated, but a subclass that implements the abstract methods of its parent class *can* be instantiated.

Public, Private, or Protected?

Java methods can be public, protected, or private. Unlike other languages, every Java method is a virtual method. A class can contain one or more constructors because they have different signatures (i.e., the set of parameters and their types).

Variables can also be public or private; other keywords for variables include `static`, `final`, and `transient`. If a variable is not initialized, the Java compiler assigns it a value that depends on its type: a variable of type `int` is initialized to 0, a variable of type `String` is initialized to null, and so forth.

The keyword *public* exposes properties and methods, whereas the keyword *private* restricts access to the class itself. The keyword *protected* limits access to the internals of a class to its subclasses as well as the class itself.

Here are some examples of using the `private` and `public` keywords:

```
private String fname = "Dave";
public String getName() { return fname; }
public void setName(String newName) { fname = newName; }
```

The setters and getters in a class are also called *accessors* and *mutators*, respectively.

THE SCOPE OF JAVA VARIABLES

Java supports reference data types that are created during instantiation of a class.

A reference variable can refer to any object of the declared type or any compatible type (such as a subclass).

There are three types of scopes for variables in Java: `local`, `instance`, and `static`. Local variables are declared inside methods, constructors, or blocks. Instance variables are declared in a class, and they do not appear inside any methods, constructors or blocks. Listing 3.1 displays the content of `JavaVars.java` that clarifies the differences among these types of variables.

LISTING 3.1: *JavaVars.java*

```
public class JavaVars
{
    // one x1 for all instances:
    public static int x1 = 10;

    // separate x2 for each instance:
    public int x2 = 20;

    public void display()
    {
        // local x3 not accessible from other methods:
        int x3 = 30;

        System.out.println("Display x1 = "+x1);
        System.out.println("Display x2 = "+x2);
        System.out.println("Display x3 = "+x3);
    }

    public static void main (String args[])
    {
        JavaVars jv1 = new JavaVars();
        System.out.println("Invoking display from jv1");
        jv1.display();

        JavaVars jv2 = new JavaVars();
        jv2.x1 = 1000;
        jv2.x2 = 345;
        System.out.println("Invoking display from jv2");
        jv2.display();

        System.out.println("Invoking display from jv1");
        jv1.display();
    }
}
```

Listing 3.1 defines the class JavaVars, along with the static variable x1, the class variable x2, and the local variable x3, initialized with the values 10, 20, and 30, respectively.

Listing 3.1 also defines the public method display() that displays the values of the variables x1, x2, and x3. Note that the value of x3 can be displayed because it's defined as a local variable in the display() method.

Next, the main() method initializes the variable jv1 as an instance of the JavaVars class, and when jv1.display() is invoked, you can see that the x1 and x2 have their original values.

The next portion of the main() method initializes the variable jv2 as an instance of the JavaVars class, after which x1 and x2 are updated with this code snippet:

```
jv2.x1 = 1000;
jv2.x2 = 345;
```

Next, `jv2.display()` is invoked and you can see that x1 and x2 have the values 1000 and 345, respectively. However, when `jv1.display()` is invoked, you can see that x1 retains its updated value of 1000 because x1 is a *static* variable, but the value of x2 has "reverted" to 20 because x2 is an *instance* variable, which means that modifying its value in instance `jv1` is independent from modifying its value in instance `jv2`.

Launch the code in Listing 3.1 and you will see the following output:

```
Invoking display from jv1
Display x1 = 10
Display x2 = 20
Display x3 = 30
Invoking display from jv2
Display x1 = 1000
Display x2 = 345
Display x3 = 30
Invoking display from jv1
Display x1 = 1000
Display x2 = 20
Display x3 = 30
```

Now that you understand the differences among static, instance, and local variables, the next subsection provides more details regarding static methods.

Static Methods

Static variables are declared in the same manner as instance variables, but with the `static` keyword. If you declare a method as `static`, that method can only update static variables; however, static variables can be updated in non-static methods. A key point about static methods is that you can reference a static method without instantiating an object. For example, the code snippet `MyClass.myStaticMethod(userId)` invokes the static method `myStaticMethod()`, with the parameter `userId` that has the required type, that is defined in the class `MyClass`.

On the other hand, non-static methods are only available through an instance of a class. Keep in mind the following points about `static` methods:

- They can only call other static methods.
- They can only access static data.
- The same method occurs in all class instances.
- They do not have a `this` reference

Listing 3.2 displays the content of `StaticMethod.java` that illustrates how to define and then invoke a static method in a `Java` class.

LISTING 3.2: StaticMethod.java

```
public class StaticMethod
{
    // a non-static method
    public void display1()
```

```
   {
      System.out.println("Inside display1");
   }

   // a static method:
   public static void display2()
   {
      System.out.println("Inside display2");
   }

   public static void main (String args[])
   {
      System.out.println("Inside main()");

      // cannot invoke non-static method:
    //StaticMethod.display1();

      // this works correctly:
      StaticMethod.display2();

      // this works correctly:
      StaticMethod sm = new StaticMethod();
      sm.display1();
   }
}
```

Listing 3.2 defines the class StaticMethod and the non-static method display1() as well as the static method display2(). Hence, the main() method can invoke the display2() method directly, without an instance of the StaticMethod class. Next, the main() method initializes the variable sm as an instance of the StaticMethod class, after which sm invokes the method display1(), which is a non-static method.

Other Static Types

As you saw in the previous section, a static method in a Java class can be invoked without instantiating an object. In addition, you can define a static Java class that only contains static methods, each of which is invoked without instantiating an object.

A *static block* (also called a static initialization block) is a set of instructions that is invoked once when a Java class is loaded into memory. A static block is used for initialization before object construction, as shown here:

```
class MyClass
{
   static int x;
   int y;

   // this is a static block:
   static {
      x = 123;
      System.out.println("static block executed");
   }

   public static void main(String[] args) {}
}
```

Compile and launch the code in the preceding class and you will see the following output:

```
static block executed
```

The next portion of this chapter shows you how to define getters and setters (also called accessors and mutators, respectively).

WHAT ARE ACCESSORS AND MUTATORS?

In essence, an accessor returns a value from a "get" method and a mutator updates a value (or multiple values) in a "set" method.

The example in this section shows you how to define a Java class that represents only two properties of a person, the first name and last name, to illustrate how to invoke the other methods in this class. A real-life class would contain many other attributes, and after you finish reading this example, you will be able to easily extend this code to a realistic example.

Listing 3.3 displays the content of Person.java that contains two private String variables for keeping track of a person's first name and last name, along with the methods that enable you to access the first name and last name of any person.

LISTING 3.3: Person.java

```java
public class Person
{
    private String firstName;
    private String lastName;

    public Person(String firstName, String lastName)
    {
        this.firstName = firstName;
        this.lastName  = lastName;
    }

    public String getFirstName()
    {
        return(this.firstName);
    }

    public String getLastName()
    {
        return(this.lastName);
    }

    public static void main (String args[])
    {
        Person p1 = new Person("John", "Smith");
        Person p2 = new Person("Jane", "Andrews");

        System.out.println("My name is "+
                    p1.getFirstName()+" "+
                    p1.getLastName());
```

```
System.out.println("My name is "+
                   p2.getFirstName()+" "+
                   p2.getLastName());
    }
}
```

Listing 3.3 defines the class `Person` and a `main()` method that initializes the variables `p1` and `p2` as instances of the `Person` class, but with different values in the constructor. The next portion of the `main()` method displays the contents of the `p1` and `p2` variables:

```
My name is John Smith
My name is Jane Andrews
```

You can enhance the code in Listing 3.3 to read a list of names that are stored in an `ASCII` file, a `CSV` file, an `XML` file, or even a `JSON` string that is returned by a Web service.

A JAVA CLASS WITHOUT ACCESSORS

This section shows you how to populate `Java` arrays with integer values and decimal values and then calculate the sum and average of the contents of those arrays. Pay close attention to the value of the average of an array of decimal numbers and compare that average value with the average of the integer portion of an array of decimal numbers.

Listing 3.4 displays the content of `ArrayExamples1.java` that calculates the sum and the average of an array of decimal numbers, as well as an array of integer numbers.

LISTING 3.4: ArrayExamples1.java

```
public class ArrayExamples
{
   public static void main(String args[])
   {
      String[] names = {"Tic", "Tac", "Toe"};

      // display the contents of the names array:
      for(int i=0; i<names.length; i++)
      {
         System.out.println("Name "+(i+1)+": "+names[i]);
      }

      int arraySize = 12;
      int maxCelsius = 40;
      double intSumCelsius = 0;
      double intAvgCelsius = 0;
      double dblSumCelsius = 0.0;
      double dblAvgCelsius = 0.0;

      double[] celsiusValues = new double[arraySize];
      int[] celsiusValues2 = new int[arraySize];
```

```
// initialize with random numeric values
for(int i=0; i<arraySize; i++)
{
    celsiusValues[i]  = maxCelsius*Math.random();
    celsiusValues2[i] = (int)celsiusValues[i];
}

// calculate the sum of the elements in the arrays
for(int i=0; i<arraySize; i++)
{
    intSumCelsius += celsiusValues2[i];
    dblSumCelsius += celsiusValues[i];
}

dblAvgCelsius = dblSumCelsius/arraySize;
intAvgCelsius = (int)(intSumCelsius/arraySize);

System.out.println("Total Celsius   "+dblSumCelsius);
System.out.println("Avg Celsius:    "+dblAvgCelsius);
System.out.println("Total Celsius2: "+intSumCelsius);
System.out.println("Avg Celsius2:   "+intAvgCelsius);
System.out.println();
    }
}
```

Listing 3.4 defines the class `ArrayExamples1` and a `main()` method that initializes the arrays `celsiusValues` and `celsiusValues2` that contain randomly generated floating point values and integer values, respectively. The next section of code calculates the sum of the values in the arrays `celsiusValues` and `celsiusValues2`.

The next portion of code displays the sum of the values in the arrays `celsiusValues` and `celsiusValues2`. Finally, the strings in the `names` array are defined at the top of Listing 3.4. Launch the code in Listing 3.4 and you will see the following output:

```
Name 1: Tic
Name 2: Tac
Name 3: Toe
Total Celsius   249.4551395046531
Avg Celsius:    20.787928292054424
Total Celsius2: 243.0
Avg Celsius2:   20.0
```

REFACTORING CODE WITH ACCESSOR METHODS

Let's modify the code in Listing 3.4 by defining several methods that perform various calculations that are currently performed inside the `main()` method.

Listing 3.5 displays the content of `ArrayExamples2.java` that is based on `ArrayExamples.java`, rewritten to include private variables and private methods.

LISTING 3.5: ArrayExamples2.java

```java
public class ArrayExamples2
{
   private int arraySize = 12;
   private int maxCelsius = 40;
   private double intSumCelsius = 0;
   private double intAvgCelsius = 0;
   private double dblSumCelsius = 0.0;
   private double dblAvgCelsius = 0.0;

   private double[] celsiusValues = new double[arraySize];
   private int[] celsiusValues2 = new int[arraySize];
   private String[] names = {"Tic", "Tac", "Toe"};

   private void initializeArrays()
   {
      // initialize arrays with random values
      for(int i=0; i<arraySize; i++)
      {
         celsiusValues[i]  = maxCelsius*Math.random();
         celsiusValues2[i] = (int)celsiusValues[i];
      }
   }

   private void calculateTotals()
   {
      // calculate the array sums
      for(int i=0; i<arraySize; i++)
      {
         intSumCelsius += celsiusValues2[i];
         dblSumCelsius += celsiusValues[i];
      }

      dblAvgCelsius = dblSumCelsius/arraySize;
      intAvgCelsius = (int)(intSumCelsius/arraySize);
   }

   private void displayCelsiusResults()
   {
      System.out.println("Total Celsius    "+dblSumCelsius);
      System.out.println("Avg Celsius:     "+dblAvgCelsius);
      System.out.println("Total Celsius2: "+intSumCelsius);
      System.out.println("Avg Celsius2:    "+intAvgCelsius);
      System.out.println();
   }

   private void displayNames()
   {
      // display the contents of the names array:
      for(int i=0; i<names.length; i++)
      {
         System.out.println("Name "+(i+1)+": "+names[i]);
      }
   }
}
```

```
public static void main(String args[])
{
    ArrayExamples2 ae2 = new ArrayExamples2();

    ae2.initializeArrays();
    ae2.calculateTotals();
    ae2.displayCelsiusResults();
    ae2.displayNames();
}
}
```

Listing 3.5 defines the class `ArrayExamples2` that initializes various scalar variables, as well as three arrays of type `double`, `int`, and `String`. The next portion of Listing 3.5 defines several methods that belong to the `ArrayExamples2` class.

The `initializeArrays()` method initializes the arrays `celsiusValues` and `celsiusValues2` that contain randomly generated floating point values and integer values, respectively. The `calculateTotals()` method calculates the sum of the values in the arrays `celsiusValues` and `celsiusValues2`.

The `displayCelsiusResults()` method displays the sum of the values in the arrays `celsiusValues` and `celsiusValues2`. Finally, the `display-Names()` method displays the strings in the `names` array that is defined at the top of Listing 3.5.

The last portion of Listing 3.5 is the `main()` method, which creates an instance of the `ArrayExamples2` class and then invokes four methods that belong to this class.

Launch the code in Listing 3.5 and you will see the same output that you saw when you launched the `Java` class `ArrayExamples2` in Chapter 1:

```
Name 1: Tic
Name 2: Tac
Name 3: Toe
Total Celsius    249.4551395046531
Avg Celsius:     20.787928292054424
Total Celsius2: 243.0
Avg Celsius2:    20.0
```

DEFINING A CONSTRUCTOR AND AN ACCESSOR

Earlier in this chapter, you learned about public, private, and protected variables, and in this section you will see an example of private methods in a `Java` class.

Listing 3.6 displays the content of `ArrayExamples3.java` that is based on `ArrayExamples2.java`, rewritten to include a constructor and an accessor method.

LISTING 3.6: ArrayExamples3.java

```
public class ArrayExamples3
{
    private int arraySize = 12;
    private int maxCelsius = 40;
```

```
private double intSumCelsius = 0;
private double intAvgCelsius = 0;
private double dblSumCelsius = 0.0;
private double dblAvgCelsius = 0.0;

private double[] celsiusValues = new double[arraySize];
private int[] celsiusValues2 = new int[arraySize];
private String[] names = {"Tic", "Tac", "Toe"};

public ArrayExamples3()
{
   initializeArrays();
   calculateTotals();
   displayCelsiusResults();
   displayNames();
}

private void initializeArrays()
{
   // initialize arrays with random values
   for(int i=0; i<arraySize; i++)
   {
      celsiusValues[i]  = maxCelsius*Math.random();
      celsiusValues2[i] = (int)celsiusValues[i];
   }
}

private void calculateTotals()
{
   // calculate the array sums
   for(int i=0; i<arraySize; i++)
   {
      intSumCelsius += celsiusValues2[i];
      dblSumCelsius += celsiusValues[i];
   }

   dblAvgCelsius = dblSumCelsius/arraySize;
   intAvgCelsius = (int)(intSumCelsius/arraySize);
}

private void displayCelsiusResults()
{
   System.out.println("Total Celsius   "+dblSumCelsius);
   System.out.println("Avg Celsius:    "+dblAvgCelsius);
   System.out.println("Total Celsius2: "+intSumCelsius);
   System.out.println("Avg Celsius2:   "+intAvgCelsius);
   System.out.println();
}

private void displayNames()
{
   // display the contents of the names array:
   for(int i=0; i<names.length; i++)
   {
      System.out.println("Name "+(i+1)+": "+names[i]);
   }
}
```

```java
    public String getFirstName()
    {
       return names[0];
    }
    public static void main(String args[])
    {
       ArrayExamples3 ae3 = new ArrayExamples3();
       String name0 = ae3.getFirstName();
       System.out.println("First name: "+name0);
    }
}
```

Listing 3.6 defines the class `ArrayExamples3` and a `main()` method that initializes the variable `ae3` as an instance of the `ArrayExamples3` class. Notice that this class has the same methods that are defined in Listing 3.5. Launch the code in Listing 3.6 and you will see similar output as that for `ArrayExamples2` in the previous section:

```
Total Celsius    230.365808921479
Avg Celsius:     19.197150743456582
Total Celsius2:  224.0
Avg Celsius2:    18.0

Name 1: Tic
Name 2: Tac
Name 3: Toe
First name: Tic
```

ACCESSORS, MUTATORS, AND THE THIS KEYWORD

Listing 3.7 displays the content of `Employee.java` that illustrates how to define an accessor (also called a "getter") method and corresponding mutator (also called a "setter") method. This code sample also defines a constructor for initializing instance variables. As you will see, we use the `this` keyword (which cannot be programmatically modified in your code) to initialize class variables with the values that are provided in constructors.

LISTING 3.7: Employee.java

```java
public class Employee
{
   private String empId;
   private int grade;
   private double years;

   public Employee(String empId, int grade, double years)
   {
      System.out.println("Local empId:     "+empId);
      System.out.println("Instance empId: "+this.empId);

      this.empId = empId;
      this.grade = grade;
      this.years = years;

      System.out.println("Instance empId: "+this.empId);
```

```
    // the following pair of code snippets show you two
    // ways to invoke the setGrade() method but they are
    // redundant: this.grade has already been initialized
    this.setGrade(grade);
    setGrade(grade);
  }

  public void setGrade(int grade)
  {
    this.grade = grade;
  }

  public static void main (String args[])
  {
    Employee emp1 = new Employee("2000", 10, 5);
    int grade1 = emp1.getGrade();
    System.out.println("Grade: "+grade1);

    emp1.setGrade(18);
    int grade2 = emp1.getGrade();
    System.out.println("Grade: "+grade2);

    // invalid code because non-static variables
    // cannot be referenced in a static context:
  //this.empId = "1234";
  }
}
```

Listing 3.7 defines the class `Employee` and a `main()` method that initializes the variable `emp1` as an instance of the `Employee` class. Notice how the constructor of the `Employee` class contains three parameters: a year, a grade, and years of experience. The constructor initializes the corresponding private instance variables via the `this` keyword with this code:

```
this.empId = empId;
this.grade = grade;
this.years = years;
```

In the preceding code block, the `this` keyword initializes the three variables of the current instance with the values of the parameters that are specified in the constructor. The three variables on the left of the equals sign in the preceding code block are *instance* variables, whereas the three variables on the right of the equals sign in the preceding code block are parameters that are specified in the method definition. Alternatively, you can also define the constructor in Listing 3.7 with the following coding style:

```
public Employee(String empIdV, int gradeV, double yearsV)
{
  empId = empIdV;
  grade = gradeV;
  years = yearsV;
}
```

However, the preceding coding style is more tedious than the code block for the constructor in Listing 3.7; alternatively, the latter is easier to modify if you need to perform a global search/replace operation.

As a distant comparison, if you have experience as a C or C++ developer, you might remember discussions regarding the use of an underscore "_" to indicate a private variable. The majority of developers use the "_" as a prefix (such as `_empId`), but some developers are adamant about using an underscore as a suffix (such as `empId_`).

Regardless of your preferred coding style, be aware of different coding styles, just in case you need to work with (or debug or enhance) other people's code.

The next section of code invokes the `getGrade()` method that returns the grade level of the employee, followed by an invocation of the `setGrade()` method that sets the grade level to 18. Next, the `getGrade()` method is invoked again, just to verify that the `setGrade()` method was executed successfully.

Admittedly, this code sample does very little: after instantiating an `Employee` instance with initial values of 2000, 10, and 5, for the `empId`, `grade`, and `years`, respectively, the code displays the value of `grade` and updates the value of `grade`. A more complete example would specify (at least some) accessors and mutators for every parameter that is listed in the constructor. Now launch the code in Listing 3.7 and you will see the following output:

```
Local empId:    2000
Instance empId: none
Instance empId: 2000
Grade: 10
Grade: 18
```

In `HelloWorld5.java`, you see how to use the `this` keyword to invoke a constructor. You can also use the `this` keyword in static blocks, which can initialize every parameter that is listed in the constructor.

ARRAYS OF CLASSES

This section shows you two ways in which you can define an array of Java classes. The preferred way involves the use of Java packages, which we'll postpone until later in this chapter. Another (albeit less elegant) solution involves defining a nested class. In this section we'll use the shorter code sample `Employee.java` because the code will be more succinct, and afterward you can add the additional parameters that are listed in `LongEmployee.java`.

Listing 3.8 displays the content of `ArrEmployees.java` that illustrates how to instantiate an array of `Employee` objects.

LISTING 3.8: ArrEmployees.java

```java
public class ArrEmployees
{
    class Employee
    {
        private String empId;
```

```
        private int grade;
        private double years;

        public Employee(String empId, int grade, double
        years)
        {
            this.empId = empId;
            this.grade = grade;
            this.years = years;
        }

        public void setGrade(int grade)
        {
            this.grade = grade;
        }

        public int getGrade()
        {
            return(this.grade);
        }
    }

    public ArrayEmployees()
    {
        Employee[] empList = new Employee[3];

        String[] ids = {"1000", "2000", "3000"};
        int[] grades = {10, 11, 12};
        int[] years  = {2, 3, 4};

        for(int i=0; i<ids.length; i++) {
            empList[i] = new Employee(ids[i],grades[i],years
            [i]);
        }

        for(int i=0; i<empList.length; i++)
        {
            Employee emp = empList[i];
            int grade = emp.getGrade();
            System.out.println("Grade for emp #"+(i+1)+":
            "+grade);
        }
    }

    public static void main (String args[])
    {
        ArrayEmployees arrEmps = new ArrayEmployees();
    }
}
```

Listing 3.8 defines the class ArrayEmployees that contains the definition of the class Employee. Now launch the code in Listing 3.8 and you will see the following output:

```
Grade for emp #1: 10
Grade for emp #2: 11
Grade for emp #3: 12
```

Notice the files that are generated alongside the class:

```
ArrayEmployees.java
ArrayEmployees.class
ArrayEmployees$Employee.class
```

STATIC METHODS

Static methods can be invoked directly from a Java class, whereas non-static methods can only be invoked from an instance of a Java class. For example, if staticMethodM() is a *static* method of class classB, then the following statement is legal:

```
classB.staticMethodM();
```

However, if nonStaticMethodM() is a *non-static* method of class classB, then the following statement is legal:

```
Class B b = new ClassB();
b.nonStaticMethodM();

//this is illegal:
classB.nonStaticMethodM();
```

Every instance of a class contains a copy of an instance variable, but only *one* copy of a static variable is available to all instances of a class. If a static variable is modified in one instance, that modified value is available to *all* the other instances, including instances that are created after a static variable has been modified. Hence, if x, y, and z are static variables in a class, and their values are modified, then the *modified* values are available in all instances of the given class.

Keep in mind the following distinction: instance variables are initialized when an instance is created, whereas class variables are initialized when the class is created.

Listing 3.9 displays the content of DataTypesVars.java that contains various primitive data types and variables.

LISTING 3.9: DataTypeVars.java

```
public class DataTypesVars
{
    // one static variable
    static int club = 5;

    // four class variables
    int length = 4;
    int myInt = 123;
    double myDouble = 123.4;
    double total = 10.0;

    public DataTypesVars() {}

    public void calculations()
```

```
{
    // two local variables
    double dbl2 = myDouble/length;
    int myAvg  = (int)(total/length);

    System.out.println("length:  "+(++length));
    System.out.println("dbl2:    "+dbl2);
    System.out.println("myAvg:   "+myAvg);
    System.out.println();
}

public static void printClub()
{
    // accessing a non-static variable
    // will cause a compilation error
    System.out.println("club:    "+(++club));
}

public static void main(String args[])
{
    DataTypesVars.printClub();
    DataTypesVars dtv1 = new DataTypesVars();
    dtv1.calculations();

    DataTypesVars.printClub();
    DataTypesVars dtv2 = new DataTypesVars();
    dtv2.calculations();
}
}
```

Listing 3.9 defines the class `DataTypesVars` and a `main()` method that invokes the static method `printClub()` that contains a `System.out.println()` statement to display the *pre-incremented* value of the `club` variable.

The next section of the `main()` method initializes the variable `dtv1` as an instance of the `DataTypesVars` class and then invokes the `calculations()` method to display the values of the scalar variables that are declared at the top of this listing. The final code block in the `main()` method also invokes the `calculations()` method and then displays the value of the variable `dtv2`. The output from Listing 3.9 is here:

```
club:    6
length:  5
dbl2:    24.68
myAvg:   2

club:    7
length:  5
dbl2:    24.68
myAvg:   2
```

Notice that the value of the static variable `club` is different in `dtv1` and `dtv2`. However, the non-static variable `length` is incremented inside the method `calculations()`, but its value is the same in `dtv1` and `dtv2`.

STATIC CODE BLOCKS

Earlier in this chapter, you saw a simple example of defining a static block in a Java class. However, we did not specify how to access a variable in a static code block and when it's possible to update the value of a variable in a static code block.

Listing 3.10 displays the content of StaticBlock.java that illustrates how to define a static code block (shown in bold) and how to access and update a variable that is initialized in a static code block.

LISTING 3.10: StaticBlock.java

```java
public class StaticBlock
{
    private static int zz = 3;

    static {
      zz = 100;
    }
    public static void display()
    {
       System.out.println("Inside display zz = "+zz);
       update();

       // illegal use of 'this':
       //this.update();
    }
    public static void update()
    {
       // illegal use of 'this':
       //this.zz = 1234;

       zz = 1234;
       System.out.println("Inside update zz = "+zz);
    }
    public static void main (String args[])
    {
       // both are illegal invocations:
       //this.display();
       //this.zz = 1234;

       StaticBlock sb = new StaticBlock();
       sb.display();

       System.out.println("Inside main zz = "+zz);

       zz = 7777;
       System.out.println("Inside main zz = "+zz);
    }
}
```

Listing 3.10 defines the class StaticBlock that consists of a static block, two static methods, and a main() method that initializes the variable sb as an instance of the StaticBlock class. Notice that the this keyword in the `main()` method is not allowed, but you *can* update the value of `zz` directly. Let's trace the output from Listing 3.10 that's shown below:

```
Inside display zz = 100
Inside update zz = 1234
Inside main zz = 1234
Inside main zz = 7777
length: 5
```

As you can see, the initial value of `zz` is immediately replaced by the value 100 that is assigned in the static code block. Next, the `sb` variable invokes the static method `display()` that displays the value of 100 for `zz`. The `display()` method then invokes the static method `update()` that sets the value of `zz` to 1234 and also displays this value.

Returning to the `main()` method, we see that the value of 1234 for `zz` is still true, and then `zz` is updated to 7777, which is the value displayed by the final `print()` statement.

Although the preceding code is admittedly somewhat contrived, its purpose is to show you various legal (and illegal) ways to modify a variable that has been initialized in a static block.

The next section shows you how to instantiate `Java` classes and how to define methods that belong to those classes.

A SECOND "HELLO WORLD" EXAMPLE

Listing 3.11 displays the content of `HelloWorld2.java` that prints the string "Hello World" from the constructor of the class `HelloWorld2`.

LISTING 3.11: HelloWorld2.java

```java
public class HelloWorld2
{
    public HelloWorld2()
    {
        System.out.println("Hello World from HelloWorld2");
    }

    public static void main (String args[])
    {
        HelloWorld2 hw = new HelloWorld2();
    }
}
```

Listing 3.11 defines the class `HelloWorld2`, along with a method called a *constructor* whose name matches the name of the class (in this case, it is `HelloWorld2`). Notice that the constructor contains the same `print()` statement that was previously located in the `main()` method. The `main()` method contains the following code snippet:

```java
HelloWorld2 hw = new HelloWorld2();
```

The preceding code snippet instantiates an object called `hw` from the class `HelloWorld2`. Whenever you instantiate an object, the default constructor is executed, which in this case contains a `print()` statement.

Open a command shell and type the following command to compile the code in Listing 3.11:

```
javac HelloWorld2.java
```

The preceding command creates the file `HelloWorld2.class` that contains bytecode. Launch this new class with the following command:

```
java HelloWorld2
```

The output from the preceding command is here:

```
Hello World from HelloWorld2
```

You can also define a class with non-constructor methods, as shown in the next section.

A THIRD "HELLO WORLD" EXAMPLE

Listing 3.12 displays the content of `HelloWorld3.java` that prints the string "Hello World" from a class.

LISTING 3.12: HelloWorld3.java

```
public class HelloWorld3
{
    public HelloWorld3() {}

    public void sayHello()
    {
        System.out.println("Hello World from HelloWorld3");
    }

    public static void main (String args[])
    {
        HelloWorld3 hw = new HelloWorld3();
        hw.sayHello();
    }
}
```

Listing 3.12 defines the class `HelloWorld3` with an empty constructor, as well as a `main()` method that initializes the variable `hw3` as an instance of the `HelloWorld3` class. The method `sayHello()` is invoked to print a text message. Launch the code in Listing 3.12 and you will see the following output:

```
Hello World from HelloWorld3
```

You can also define a class that contains multiple constructors with one or more parameters, as shown in the next section.

A FOURTH "HELLO WORLD" EXAMPLE

Listing 3.13 displays the content of `HelloWorld4.java` that prints the string "Hello World" from a class.

LISTING 3.13: HelloWorld4.java

```java
public class HelloWorld4
{
   public HelloWorld4()
   {
      System.out.println("Constructor1");
      sayHello();
   }

   public HelloWorld4(int x)
   {
      System.out.println("Constructor2");
      sayHello();
   }

   public HelloWorld4(int x, int y)
   {
      System.out.println("Constructor3");
      sayHello();
   }

   public void sayHello()
   {
      System.out.println("Hello World from HelloWorld4");
   }

   public static void main (String args[])
   {
      HelloWorld4 hw1 = new HelloWorld4();
      HelloWorld4 hw2 = new HelloWorld4(10);
      HelloWorld4 hw3 = new HelloWorld4(10, 40);
   }
}
```

Listing 3.13 defines the class `HelloWorld4` and several constructors. As you can see, the constructors are defined with zero or more parameters, and each constructor invokes the method called `sayHello()` that contains a `print()` statement.

This time, the `main()` method contains *three* instances of the `HelloWorld4` class that are created in the following code block:

```java
HelloWorld4 hw1 = new HelloWorld4();
HelloWorld4 hw2 = new HelloWorld4(10);
HelloWorld4 hw3 = new HelloWorld4(10, 40);
```

The preceding code block first instantiates an object called `hw1` from the class `HelloWorld3` without any arguments, which means that the empty constructor is executed.

Next, the object called `hw2` is instantiated, and this time the value 10 is supplied as an argument, which matches the second constructor in Listing 3.13.

Finally, the preceding code block instantiates an object called `hw3` from the class `HelloWorld3` with two arguments, which matches the third constructor in Listing 3.13.

Each constructor in Listing 3.13 prints a string and then invokes the method `sayHello()` that prints the string "Hello World from HelloWorld4." Launch the code in Listing 3.13 and you will see the following output:

```
Constructor1
Hello World from HelloWorld4
Constructor2
Hello World from HelloWorld4
Constructor3
Hello World from HelloWorld4
```

Note: The parameters in the second and third constructors are not used in the code because the purpose of the code is simply to illustrate how to define constructors with zero or more parameters.

The next code example in this sequence of examples illustrates how to invoke a constructor from another constructor.

A FIFTH "HELLO WORLD" EXAMPLE

Listing 3.14 displays the content of `HelloWorld5.java` that prints the string "Hello World" from a `Java` class.

LISTING 3.14: HelloWorld5.java

```java
public class HelloWorld5
{
    public HelloWorld5()
    {
        this(10);
        System.out.println("Constructor1");
    }

    public HelloWorld5(int x)
    {
        this(10, 20);
        System.out.println("Constructor2");
    }

    public HelloWorld5(int x, int y)
    {
        sayHello();
        System.out.println("Constructor3");
    }
```

```
public void sayHello()
{
   System.out.println("Hello World from HelloWorld5");
}

public static void main (String args[])
{
   HelloWorld5 hw1 = new HelloWorld5();
   HelloWorld5 hw2 = new HelloWorld5(10);
   HelloWorld5 hw3 = new HelloWorld5(10, 40);
}
}
```

Listing 3.14 defines the class HelloWorld5, along with several constructors with zero or more parameters. Notice that the constructor with zero parameters uses the this keyword to invoke the constructor with one parameter. Similarly, the constructor with one parameter uses the this keyword to invoke the constructor with two parameters, and the latter invokes the method called sayHello() that contains a print() statement.

The main() method creates three instances of the class HelloWorld5 in the following code block:

```
HelloWorld4 hw1 = new HelloWorld4();
HelloWorld4 hw2 = new HelloWorld4(10);
HelloWorld4 hw3 = new HelloWorld4(10, 40);
```

The preceding code block is identical to the corresponding code block in HelloWorld4.java in Listing 3.14. However, the output is quite different, as you can see (can you guess what happens without looking at the output?):

```
Hello World from HelloWorld5
Constructor3
Constructor2
Constructor1
Hello World from HelloWorld5
Constructor3
Constructor2
Hello World from HelloWorld5
Constructor3
```

Once again, the parameters in the second and third constructors are not used in the code because the purpose of the code is simply to illustrate how to define constructors with zero or more parameters.

The this keyword appears before the print() statement (or any other code) in the constructors, otherwise you will see the following error message during compilation:

```
call to this must be first statement in constructor
```

This concludes the discussion of creating Java classes involving multiple constructors.

JAVA ANONYMOUS INNER CLASSES

A Java *inner class* is a class that is defined in the same file as another class. Specifically, if ClassA.java contains the definition of ClassB, then ClassB is an inner class. Listing 3.15 displays the content of Regular.java that illustrates how to define an inner class.

LISTING 3.15: Regular.java

```
public class Regular
{
    class Nested {
        public Nested() {
            System.out.println("Inside Nested constructor");
        }
    }

    class Nested2 {
        public Nested2() {
            System.out.println("Inside Nested2 constructor");
        }
    }

    public Regular()
    {
        System.out.println("Inside Regular constructor");
        Nested nest = new Nested();
        Nested nest2 = new Nested2();
    }

    public static void main (String args[])
    {
        System.out.println("Inside main()");
        Regular reg = new Regular();
    }
}
```

Listing 3.15 defines the class Regular and the inner classes Nested and Nested2. Notice that the latter two classes do not contain the public keyword. As a reminder, a file that defines a class cannot contain more than one public class: all other class definitions are inner classes. Now compile the code in Listing 3.15 and you will find the following files in your directory:

```
Regular.java
Regular.class
Regular$Nested2.class
Regular$Nested.class
```

Launch the code and you will see the following output:

```
Inside main()
Inside Regular constructor
Inside Nested constructor
Inside Nested constructor2
```

JAVA NAMED INNER CLASSES

Listing 3.16 displays the content of Regular2.java that illustrates how to define a named inner class (that is also static).

LISTING 3.16: Regular2.java

```java
public class Regular2
{
    // named inner class
    private static class Nested {
        public Nested() {
            System.out.println("Inside Nested constructor");
        }
    }

    // named inner class
    private class Nested2 {
        public Nested2() {
            System.out.println("Inside Nested2 constructor");
        }
    }

    public Regular2()
    {
        System.out.println("Inside Regular2 constructor");
        Nested nest = new Nested();
        Nested nest2 = new Nested2();
    }

    public static void main (String args[])
    {
        System.out.println("Inside main()");
        Regular reg2 = new Regular2();

        System.out.println("Instantiating Nested inside
        main()");
        Nested nest = new Nested();

        // a non-static variable cannot be
        // referenced from a static context:
        //Nested2 nest2 = new Nested2();
    }
}
```

Listing 3.16 defines the class Regular2 and the private static inner class Nested and the private class Nested2. Now launch the code and you will see the following output:

```
Inside main()
Inside Regular2 constructor
Inside Nested constructor
Inside Nested2 constructor
Instantiating Nested inside main()
Inside Nested constructor
```

ANONYMOUS CLASSES VERSUS NAMED INNER CLASSES

As you know, a `Java` class can extend a class and implement an *arbitrary* number of interfaces. By contrast, an anonymous inner class can implement *only one* interface. In addition, *anonymous* inner classes are private (i.e., other public classes cannot access them), whereas *named* inner classes can be used only by the enclosing public class.

Be careful not to inadvertently mistake a named inner class as a class that's used in multiple locations (which is much less likely to happen) with an anonymous inner class. As a suggestion, use anonymous inner classes when they are used *only once* (such as an event handler for a button click in a `GUI`), and use named inner classes if they are used *more than once* in your code. Anonymous classes in Java can have an initializer such as the following:

```
{
    super.foo(finalVariable+this.bar);
}
```

Limitations of Anonymous Classes

Although anonymous classes have some advantages, they also have limitations, as listed below:

- they cannot be reused
- they cannot have anything static in their definition
- their fields cannot be inspected in Eclipse
- they cannot be used as a type
- they cannot be located using the class name in Eclipse
- they do not have a name, so they cannot have a constructor
- they cannot change the values of any included class members

By contrast, *named* inner classes do not have the preceding limitations.

Incidentally, here is a scenario in which *non-static* inner classes can be problematic. Suppose that an outer class is not serializable, whereas an inner class *is* serializable. In this situation, there will be an attempt to serialize the outer class but this will fail (and therefore more time will be spent debugging your code).

Since anonymous classes cannot have a constructor, how would you pass non-constructor variables from class B to A, where B is a subclass of A? One possibility involves the use of a (static) named inner class.

PRIVATE CONSTRUCTORS (WHY?)

Thus far, you have seen only public constructors, and you might think that a private constructor serves no useful purpose. However, a private constructor is useful when you want to ensure that only one instance of a class is created, which is also known as the *singleton pattern*.

Listing 3.17 displays the content of `SingleInstance.java` that illustrates how to define a private constructor in a class.

LISTING 3.17: SingleInstance.java

```
class PrivateConstructor
{
    static PrivateConstructor instance = null;
    public int prime = 37;

    // private constructor is inaccessible outside the class
    private PrivateConstructor() {}

    // A method to construct an instance:
    static public PrivateConstructor getInstance()
    {
        // create an instance only once:
        if (instance == null)
        {
            instance = new PrivateConstructor();
        }

        return instance;
    }
}

public class SingleInstance
{
    public SingleInstance() {}

    public static void main(String args[])
    {
        PrivateConstructor inst1 = PrivateConstructor.getInstance();
        PrivateConstructor inst2 = PrivateConstructor.getInstance();

        System.out.println("Before update:");
        System.out.println("Value of inst1.prime = " + inst1.prime);
        System.out.println("Value of inst2.prime = " + inst2.prime);

        inst1.prime = inst1.prime + 64;

        System.out.println("After  update:");
        System.out.println("Value of inst1.prime = " + inst1.prime);
        System.out.println("Value of inst2.prime = " + inst2.prime);
    }
}
```

Listing 3.17 defines the inner class `PrivateConstructor` with a *private* constructor in which the variable `instance` has an initial value of `null`. The variable `instance` is initialized only once, which ensures that there is only one instance of the `PrivateConstructor` class.

Listing 3.17 also defines the class `SingleInstance`, a public constructor, and a `main()` method that initializes the variables `inst1` and `inst2` as instances of the class `PrivateConstructor`.

Next, two `print()` statements display the value of the integer variable prime (a public variable in the `PrivateConstructor` class) whose initial value is 37. Both instance variables `inst1` and `inst2` have the value 37 for the variable prime.

The next portion of the `main()` method adds 64 to the value of the variable prime, and two `print()` statements display its updated value. Launch the code in Listing 3.17 and you will see the following output:

```
Before update:
Value of inst1.prime = 37
Value of inst2.prime = 37
After  update:
Value of inst1.prime = 101
Value of inst2.prime = 101
```

THE JAVA IMPORT STATEMENT

You can import compiled Java classes into your Java class using the `import` statement. For example, suppose that the file `MyClass.java` is in the package `com.acme.dept` and you want to import the class `Employee` whose package is `com.acme.employees`. The file `MyClass.java` *must* appear in this directory structure:

```
<your-top-directory>.com/acme/dept/MyClass.java
```

The file `MyClass.java` will contain the following code:

```
package com.acme.dept;
import com.acme.employees.Employee;

public class MyClass extends MyBase implements BaseInfo
{
    private Employee emp;

    // code goes here
}
```

The preceding code block contains a reference to the imported `Employee` class because presumably you are going to do something with that class in the class `MyClass`.

You can easily import all the Java classes that belong to a package. For example, the following `import` statement imports all the classes in the `com.acme.employees` package:

```
import com.acme.employees.*;
```

The compiler will import *only* the Java classes that are needed for your code, so you can use the wildcard statement or the explicit Java classes in a package. However, in many cases, it's probably a better coding practice to explicitly import the Java classes that are needed for your program instead of relying on the compiler.

THE JAVA PACKAGE STATEMENT

Java supports the `package` construct that is available in other languages, such as Ada. Note that a package name *must* appear as the first non-comment line in a Java file. A package is a convenient way to disambiguate a Java file with the same name that appears in more than one location. This feature is similar to the use of namespaces in XML.

For example, suppose you have one Java file called `Employee.java` class in the package `com.acme.employees`, a second Java file called `Employee.java` in the package is `com.mycorp.employees`, and a third Java file called `Employee.java` that does not belong to a package. Obviously, you must place these files in different directories. Specifically, place each `Employee.java` file in a subdirectory that reflects the structure of its package. In the preceding scenario, you will have the following directory structure:

```
$TOP/com/acme/employees/Employee.java
$TOP/com/mycorp/employees/Employee.java
$TOP/Employee.java
```

As you can see, the preceding directory structure enables you to maintain distinct Java files that have the same filename. In fact, the preceding Java files can be in different `$TOP` directories, but for convenience, we will use the same `$TOP` directory.

You must compile a Java class from the directory that is the parent of the left-most component of its package name. In the case of our three `Employee.java` files, you compile them as follows (assuming that there are no other dependencies):

```
cd $TOP
javac com.acme.employees.Employee.java
javac com.mycorp.employees.Employee.java
javac Employee.java
```

AN EXAMPLE OF THE PACKAGE STATEMENT (1)

Earlier in this chapter, you saw an example of defining an array of instances of a Java class `Employee`, where the `Employee` class is defined as a class inside the file `ArrEmployees.java`.

In this section, you will see how to use the `package` statement to define the `Employee` class in a separate file that belongs to the same package as the `ArrEmployees` class.

Listing 3.18 displays the content of `Employee.java` that belongs to the `com.employees` package, which means that `Employee.java` must appear in the following directory structure:

```
<your-top-directory>.com/acme/dept/Employee.java
```

LISTING 3.18: Employee.java

```
package com.employees;

public class Employee
{
   private String empId;
   private int grade;
   private double years;

   public Employee(String empId, int grade, double years)
   {
      this.empId = empId;
      this.grade = grade;
      this.years = years;
   }

   public void setGrade(int grade)
   {
      this.grade = grade;
   }

   public int getGrade()
   {
      return(this.grade);
   }

   public static void main (String args[]) {}
}
```

Listing 3.17 starts with a `package` statement and then defines the class `Employee` that contains three private variables and a constructor that specifies values for those variables. The next portion of Listing 3.17 contains a setter and getter for the private variable `grade`, followed by an empty `main()` method.

Listing 3.18 displays the content of `Employee.java` that belongs to the `com.acme` package, so it must appear in the following directory structure:

```
<your-top-directory>/com/acme/Employee.java
```

LISTING 3.18: ArrEmployees.java

```
package com.acme;

import com.acme.Employee;

public class ArrayEmployees
{
   public ArrayEmployees() { }

   public static void main (String args[])
   {
      Employee[] empList = new Employee[3];

      String[] ids = {"1000", "2000", "3000"};
```

```
        int[] grades = {10, 11, 12};
        int[] years  = {2, 3, 4};

        for(int i=0; i<ids.length; i++) {
            empList[i] = new Employee(ids[i],grades[i],years
  [i]);
        }

        for(int i=0; i<empList.length; i++) {
            Employee emp = empList[i];
            int grade = emp.getGrade();
            System.out.println("Grade for emp #"+(i+1)+":
            "+grade);
        }
    }
}
```

Listing 3.18 contains only two new code snippets, both of which are shown in bold. The first code snippet is a `package` statement, and the second snippet is an `import` statement that imports the class `Employee` that is also in the same package as the `ArrEmployees` class.

Now navigate to the *parent* of the `com` subdirectory and compile the classes individually with the following pair of commands:

```
javac -d . com/acme/Employee.java
javac -d . com/acme/ArrayEmployees.java
```

Alternatively, you can compile both of the preceding classes with the following command:

```
javac -d . com/acme/*.java
```

Since the classes belong to a package, you need to prepend the package in "dotted" style to the class `ArrEmployees`. Specifically, navigate to the *parent* of the `com` subdirectory and launch `ArrEmployees` by typing the following command:

```
java com.acme.ArrayEmployees
```

You will see the following output from the preceding command:

```
Grade for emp #1: 10
Grade for emp #2: 11
Grade for emp #3: 12
```

The `javac` compiler supports many other options (not just the `-d` option for `javac`), which you can explore by typing the following command:

```
javac --help
```

Perform an online search for more information regarding the `javac` options that interest you.

AN EXAMPLE OF THE PACKAGE STATEMENT (2)

The Java class LongEmployee in a previous section will be refactored into the four Java classes Employee.java, EmpDetails.java, Person.java, and Address.java, all of which belong to the same package. In this example, the Employee entity contains one EmpDetails entity, one Person entity, and one Address entity. Thus, the Employee entity has a one-to-one relationship with the other three entities. However, it's certainly possible for the Employee entity to have a one-to-many relationship with the Address entity.

Keep in mind that the number of lines in the refactored code is slightly longer than the class LongEmployee. However, you can perform unit tests on each of the "smaller" classes independently, which makes it easier to find and fix bugs in your code. Moreover, code reuse is easier with the refactored classes than the single monolithic class LongEmployee.

Listing 3.19 displays the content of Employee.java that belongs to the com.employees package.

LISTING 3.19: Employee.java

```
package com.employees;

public class Employee
{
    private Person  person;
    private Address address;
    private EmpDetails empDetails;

    private String firstName;
    private String lastName;

    private String street;
    private String city;
    private String state;

    private String empId;
    private int grade;
    private double years;

    public Employee(String firstName, String lastName, String
    street, String city, String state, String empId, int
    grade, double years)
    {
        this.firstName = firstName;
        this.lastName  = lastName;
        this.person    = new Person(firstName, lastName);

        this.street = street;
        this.city   = city;
        this.state  = state;
        this.address = new Address(street, city, state);

        this.empId = empId;
        this.grade = grade;
```

```
         this.years = years;
         this.empDetails = new EmpDetails(empId, grade,
         years);
      }

      public Person getPerson()
      {
         return this.person;
      }

      public Address getAddress()
      {
         return this.address;
      }

      public EmpDetails getEmpDetails()
      {
         return this.empDetails;
      }

      public void printDetails()
      {
         person = this.getPerson();
         address = this.getAddress();
         empDetails = this.getEmpDetails();

         System.out.println("First Name: "+person.
         getFirstName());
         System.out.println("Last Name:  "+person.
         getLastName());
      }

      public static void main (String args[])
      {
         Employee e1 = new Employee("John", "Smith", "1234
         Main St", "Chicago", "IL", "2000", 10, 5);
         Employee e2 = new Employee("Jane", "Andrews", "1234
         Oak Ave", "Newport", "CA", "2000", 10, 5);
         e1.printDetails();
         e2.printDetails();
      }
   }
```

Listing 3.19 contains a `package` statement, and three new classes:

```
private Person  person;
private Address address;
private EmpDetails empDetails;
```

The next portion of Listing 3.19 contains the same eight private variables that are declared in `LongEmployee`. Next, a constructor takes eight parameters and performs similar initializations. However, this initialization block also instantiates three objects. Specifically, the following code snippet instantiates the object person that is of type `Person`:

```
this.person = new Person(firstName, lastName);
```

The next code snippet instantiates the object `address` that is of type `Address`:

```
this.address = new Address(street, city, state);
```

The third code snippet instantiates the object `empDetails` that is of type `empDetails`:

```
this.empDetails = new EmpDetails(empId, grade, years);
```

Listing 3.20 displays the content of `EmpDetails.java` that belongs to the `com.employees` package.

LISTING 3.20: EmpDetails.java

```
package com.employees;

public class EmpDetails
{
    private String empId;
    private int grade;
    private double years;

    public EmpDetails(String empId, int grade, double years)
    {
        this.empId = empId;
        this.grade = grade;
        this.years = years;
    }
    public void setGrade(int grade)
    {
        this.grade = grade;
    }
    public int getGrade()
    {
        return(this.grade);
    }
}
```

Listing 3.20 defines the private variables `empId`, `grade`, and `years` that are initialized with values each time that an object of type `empDetails` is instantiated.

Listing 3.21 displays the content of `Person.java` that belongs to the `com.employees` package.

LISTING 3.21: Person.java

```
package com.employees;

public class Person
{
    private String firstName;
```

```java
    private String lastName;
    public Person(String firstName, String lastName)
    {
       this.firstName = firstName;
       this.lastName  = lastName;
    }

    public String getFirstName()
    {
       return(this.firstName);
    }

    public String getLastName()
    {
       return(this.lastName);
    }
}
```

Listing 3.21 defines the private variables firstName and lastName that are initialized with values each time that an object of type EmpDetails is instantiated.

Listing 3.22 displays the content of Address.java that belongs to the com.employees package.

LISTING 3.22: Address.java

```java
package com.employees;

public class Address
{
   private String street;
   private String city;
   private String state;

   public Address(String street, String city, String state)
   {
      this.street = street;
      this.city   = city;
      this.state  = state;
   }
}
```

Listing 3.22 defines the private variables street, city, and state that are initialized with values each time that an object of type EmpDetails is instantiated.

Launch the class Employee from the directory that is two levels higher than the directory com/employees by invoking the following command:

```
java com.employees.Employee
```

The output from launching the class is shown here:

```
First Name: John
Last Name:  Smith
First Name: Jane
Last Name:  Andrews
```

CREATING JAVA JAR FILES FOR JAVA CLASS FILES

So far, you have seen examples of one-off Java classes that you can launch from the command line. However, a real application can contain dozens (even hundreds or thousands) of classes, located in various packages in multiple directories. Fortunately, you can create a JAR file containing your compiled code via the jar command.

As a simple example, the following set of steps creates a JAR file that contains the class CompareStrings from Chapter 1:

Step 1: Navigate to the directory that contains CompareStrings.
Step 2: Create a JAR file with this class file:

```
jar cvf MYCLASSES.jar CompareStrings
```

Step 3: Copy the JAR file to a directory that does not contain CompareStrings and then navigate to that directory.

Step 4: Launch CompareStrings by specifying the JAR file:

```
java -classpath MYCLASSES.jar CompareStrings
```

After you launch the preceding command, you will see the following output:

```
line1: This is a simple sentence.
line2: this is a simple sentence.

line1 and line2 are case-insensitive same
line1 is mixed case
```

Although the preceding example is trivial, you can see the usefulness of creating JAR files that contain application-related code, which can be organized in custom Java packages.

In addition, just add this JAR file to the CLASSPATH environment variable so that your application can locate any required classes, an example of which is shown here for Unix/Linux systems:

```
export CLASSPATH=$TOP/MYCLASSES.jar:$CLASSPATH
```

If you want to create a JAR file called Employee.jar that contains only the compiled Java file(s) in a directory, use the following command:

```
cd $TOP
jar cvf Employee.jar *.class
```

If you want to create a JAR file called MyBigApp.jar that contains the compiled Java file(s) in the current directory and *all* subdirectories of the current directory, which would include all the compiled Java classes in those subdirectories, invoke the following command:

```
cd $TOP
jar cvf MyBigApp.jar .
```

Once again, update the `CLASSPATH` environment with the location of the new JAR file:

```
export CLASSPATH=$TOP/MyBigApp.jar:$CLASSPATH
```

SUMMARY

This chapter started with a description of a `Java` class, as well as the differences among public, private, and protected variables and methods. You then learned about the scope of variables and the file naming convention.

Next, you learned about accessors and mutators, along with an example of a class without accessors that was later refactored to include accessors. In addition, you learned about the `this` keyword, and how to define an array of classes.

Moreover, you saw how to define class-level methods, static methods, and static blocks in `Java` code. You also learned how to instantiate objects with zero or more arguments, along with multiple constructors. Next you learned how to invoke one constructor from another constructor in a class.

Then you learned about the `package` statement and the `import` statement, as well as how to compile programs. Finally, you saw how to create JAR files that contain application-related compiled classes, which you can add to the `CLASSPATH` environment variable.

CHAPTER 4

LOOPS, ARRAYS, AND RECURSION

This chapter contains various code samples that involve `for` loops, `while` loops, arrays, and recursion in `Java`.

The first part of this chapter contains `Java` code samples with `for` loops and `while` loops. These constructs are introduced early in this chapter because the more useful code samples often contain a combination of loops and conditional logic.

The second part of this chapter contains `Java` code samples that manipulate strings, such as reversing a string and converting strings to uppercase or lowercase. This section also shows you how to work with nested loops.

The final part of this chapter shows you how to use recursion to calculate factorial values, Fibonacci numbers, the GCD (Greatest Common Divisor) of two positive integers, and the LCM (Lowest Common Multiple) of two positive integers.

Although you probably won't need to implement Euclid's algorithm as one of your daily tasks, it does provide an elegant way to calculate the greatest common divisor of two numbers, and the code is a nice example of recursion. However, you can skip this section with no loss of continuity. You can always return to this portion of the chapter when you're ready to tackle recursion.

WORKING WITH FOR LOOPS

Listing 4.1 displays the content of `ForLoops1.java` that iterates through a set of numbers and prints their values.

LISTING 4.1: ForLoops1.java

```java
public class ForLoops1
{
    private int maxCount1 = 8;
    private double sum1 = 0;

    public ForLoops1() {}

    public void calculateAverage()
    {
        for(int i=0; i<maxCount1; i++)
        {
            sum1 += i;
            System.out.println("Partial sum: "+sum1);
        }

        double avg = sum1/maxCount1;
        System.out.println("Total:    "+sum1);
        System.out.println("Average: "+avg);
    }

    public static void main(String args[])
    {
        ForLoops1 fl1 = new ForLoops1();
        fl1.calculateAverage();
    }
}
```

Listing 4.1 defines the class `ForLoops1` and a `main()` method that initializes the variable `fl1` as an instance of the `ForLoops1` class. Next, the `calculateAverage()` method (which belongs to the `ForLoops1` class) is invoked, which starts with calculating the sum of the numbers between 1 and `maxCount1` in a simple `for` loop. The last portion of the `calculateAverage()` method computes the average of the set of numbers and then prints the total and then their average. The output from Listing 4.1 is here:

```
Partial sum: 0.0
Partial sum: 1.0
Partial sum: 3.0
Partial sum: 6.0
Partial sum: 10.0
Partial sum: 15.0
Partial sum: 21.0
Partial sum: 28.0
Total:    28.0
Average: 3.5
```

DETERMINING LEAP YEARS

Listing 4.2 displays the content of `LeapYear.java` that determines whether a positive integer is a leap year. Leap years are multiples of 4, excluding centuries that are *not* a multiple of 400. Based on the preceding definition, the numbers 1700, 1800, and 1900 are *not* leap years, whereas 2000 *is* a leap year.

The code sample in this section has some nice features. First, the conditional logic is a good illustration of the usefulness of nested conditional statements. Second, observe that the definition of a leap year is described in *two comment lines* in Listing 4.2, whereas 40 lines of code are required to implement those two comment lines. Third, this code sample illustrates the importance of having a clear understanding of a task, which will make the logic of your code easier to implement, test, and debug.

If you're interested in testing your coding skills, write your own code for the determination of leap years and compare it with the content of Listing 4.2.

LISTING 4.2: LeapYear.java

```java
public class LeapYear
{
    public LeapYear() {}

    // leap years are multiples of 4 except for
    // centuries that are not multiples of 400
    public void checkYear(int year)
    {
        if(year % 4 == 0)
        {
            if(year % 100 == 0)
            {
                if(year % 400 == 0)
                {
                    System.out.println(year + " is a leap year");
                }
                else
                {
                    System.out.println(year + " is not a leap year");
                }
            }
            else
            {
                System.out.println(year + " is a leap year");
            }
        }
        else
        {
            System.out.println(year + " is not a leap year");
        }
    }

    public static void main(String args[])
    {
        LeapYear ly = new LeapYear();
        int[] years = {1234, 1900, 2000, 2020, 3000, 5588};
        for (int year : years)
        {
            ly.checkYear(year);
        }
    }
}
```

Listing 4.2 defines the class `LeapYear` that contains the method `checkYear()` that determines whether a positive integer is a leap year. If you look at the comment block near the beginning of Listing 4.2, you will see that the method `checkYear` implements the same conditional logic. Launch the code in Listing 4.2 and you will see the following output:

```
1234 is not a leap year
1900 is not a leap year
2000 is a leap year
2020 is a leap year
3000 is a leap year
5588 is a leap year
```

JAVA FOR LOOPS WITH INTEGERS

For the `Java` code in this section, remember that a variable of type `int` has a corresponding wrapper class called `Integer`. Recall that in Chapter 1, you saw an example of invoking the method `Integer.toString()` to convert an integer value to a string.

Listing 4.3 contains two types of `for` loops that show you how to display an array of integer-valued numbers.

LISTING 4.3: MyIntegers.java

```
public class MyIntegers
{
    public static void main(String[] args)
    {
        Integer[] myInts = new Integer[5];

        for(int i=0; i<5; i++)
        {
            myInts[i] = new Integer(i);
        }

        for(Integer i: myInts)
        {
            System.out.println("Integer i: "+i);
        }
    }
}
```

Listing 4.3 defines an `Integer`-based array `myInts` of integer values, followed by a `for` loop that initializes `myInts` with the `Integer`-based counterpart of the "primitive" integers from 0 to 4. The second `for` loop uses a slightly different syntax to iterate through the values in `myInts` and display their values. Launch the code in Listing 4.3 and you will see the following output:

```
Integer i: 0
Integer i: 1
Integer i: 2
Integer i: 3
Integer i: 4
```

CHECKING FOR PALINDROMES

A *palindrome* is a sequence of digits or characters that are identical when you read them on both directions (i.e., from left to right and from right to left). For example, the string BoB is a palindrome, but Bob is *not* a palindrome. Similarly, the number 12321 is a palindrome, but 1232 is not a palindrome.

Listing 4.4 displays the content of Palindromes1.java that checks if a given string or number is a palindrome.

LISTING 4.4: Palindromes1.java

```java
public class Palindromes1
{
  public Palindromes1() {}
   public void calculate(String str)
   {
      int result = 0;
      int len = str.length();

      for(int i=0; i<len/2; i++)
      {
         if(str.charAt(i) != str.charAt(len-i-1))
         {
            result = 1;
            break;
         }
      }

      if(result == 0)
      {
         System.out.println(str + ": is a palindrome");
      }
      else
      {
         System.out.println(str + ": is not a palindrome");
      }
   }

   public static void main(String args[])
   {
      String[] names = {"Dave", "BoB", "radar", "rotor"};
      int[] numbers  = {1234, 767, 1234321, -101};

      Palindromes1 pal1 = new Palindromes1();

      for (String name : names)
      {
         pal1.calculate(name);
      }

      for (int num : numbers)
      {
         pal1.calculate(Integer.toString(num));
      }
   }
}
```

Listing 4.4 defines the class `Palindromes1` that contains the method calculate to determine whether a string is a palindrome. The `main()` method defines the array names that contains a set of strings and the array `numbers` that contains a set of numbers.

Next, the `main()` method instantiates the `Palindromes1` class and then invokes the `calculate()` method with each string in the names array. Similarly, the method `calculate()` is invoked with each number in the `numbers` array by converting the numeric values to string by means of the `Integer.toString()` method. Launch the code in Listing 4.4 and you will see the following output:

```
Dave: is not a palindrome
BoB: is a palindrome
radar: is a palindrome
rotor: is a palindrome
1234: is not a palindrome
767: is a palindrome
1234321: is a palindrome
-101: is not a palindrome
```

NESTED LOOPS

Listing 4.5 displays the content of `Triangular1.java` that iterates through a set of numbers and prints their values in a triangular pattern.

LISTING 4.5: Triangular1.java

```java
public class Triangular1
{
    private int maxCount1 = 8;
    private double sum1 = 0;

    public Triangular1() {}

    public void nestedLoop()
    {
        for(int i=2; i<maxCount1; i++)
        {
            for(int j=1; j<i; j++)
            {
                System.out.print(j);
            }
            System.out.println();
        }
    }

    public static void main(String args[])
    {
        Triangular1 fl1 = new Triangular1();
        fl1.nestedLoop();
    }
}
```

Listing 4.5 defines the class `Triangular1` that contains the method `nestedLoop()` for displaying a triangular-shaped set of numbers. The `nestedLoop()` method contains an outer loop whose loop variable i iterates through the numbers from 2 to `maxCount1`, as well as an inner loop whose loop variable j iterates through the numbers from 1 to i. For each value of i in the outer loop, the inner loop displays a row of numbers, as shown here:

```
1
12
123
1234
12345
123456
```

GOLDBACH'S CONJECTURE

Goldbach's conjecture states that every even number greater than 4 can be expressed as the sum of two prime numbers. For example, $12 = 5 + 7$, $14 = 3 + 11$, $14 = 7 + 7$, $22 = 3 + 19$, $22 = 5 + 17$, and $22 = 11 + 11$, which shows you that some even numbers can be expressed as the sum of more than one pair of prime numbers. The code sample in this section will validate Goldbach's conjecture for the even numbers between 6 and 50.

Listing 4.6 displays the content of `GoldbachConjecture.java` that finds all pairs of prime numbers whose sum equals an even number.

LISTING 4.6: GoldbachConjecture.java

```java
public class GoldbachConjecture
{
    int PRIME = 1;
    int COMPOSITE = 0;

    public GoldbachConjecture() {}

    public int prime(int num)
    {
        int div = 2;

        while(div < num)
        {
            if( num % div != 0)
            {
                ++div;
            }
            else
            {
                return COMPOSITE;
            }
        }
        return PRIME;
    }
```

```java
public void findPrimeFactors(int evenNum)
{
    for (int num=3; num<=evenNum/2; num+=1)
    {
        if( (this.prime(num) == 1) && (this.prime(evenNum-
        num) == 1) )
        {
            System.out.println(
                evenNum + " = " + num + " " + " " + (evenNum-
                num));
        }
    }
}

public static void main(String args[])
{
    int upperBound = 30;

    GoldbachConjecture gbach = new GoldbachConjecture();

    for (int num=4; num<=upperBound; num+=2)
    {
        gbach.findPrimeFactors(num);
    }
}
}
```

Listing 4.6 contains a method that determines whether a number is prime. The findPrimeFactors() method will find all the pair of integers that are prime and whose sum equals a given number, which in this case is the value of the variable evenNum. The key idea is as follows: if x *and* evenNum-x are both prime, then these two numbers satisfy Goldbach's conjecture for the number evenNum. The output from Listing 4.6 is here:

```
6 = 3 + 3
8 = 3 + 5
10 = 3 + 7
10 = 5 + 5
12 = 5 + 7
14 = 3 + 11
14 = 7 + 7
16 = 3 + 13
16 = 5 + 11
18 = 5 + 13
18 = 7 + 11
20 = 3 + 17
20 = 7 + 13
22 = 3 + 19
22 = 5 + 17
22 = 11 + 11
24 = 5 + 19
24 = 7 + 17
24 = 11 + 13
26 = 3 + 23
26 = 7 + 19
26 = 13 + 13
```

```
28 = 5 + 23
28 = 11 + 17
30 = 7 + 23
30 = 11 + 19
30 = 13 + 17
```

VARIATIONS OF A BASIC FOR LOOP

The previous code samples containing a `for` loop have the same structure: initialization, logical test, and increment. This section shows you some variations that might be useful for you. The code samples are terse: most of them do not have a body, and although several of the code snippets are obvious, some of them might require you to write some code to determine their output.

Decrementing i from 5 to 0:

```
for (int i=5; i>=0; i--) { ... }
```

Incrementing i inside a `for` loop (from 0 to 5):

```
for (int i=0; i<=5;)
{
    i++;
}
```

Initializing i before a `for` loop:

```
int i=0;
for(; i < 5; i++) { ... }
```

Initializing i and j, incrementing i, and decrementing j:

```
for (i=0, j=5; i<j; i++, j--) { ... }
```

A "forever" loop (useful for user input):

```
for(;;) { ... }
```

The second `print()` statement below is invalid:

```
for(int i=0; i<5; i++)
    System.out.println("i: "+i)
System.out.println("i: "+i)
```

A `for` loop with a `break` statement:

```
for (int i=0; i<=5; i++)
{
    if(i == 3) break;
    System.out.println("i: "+i)
}
```

A `for` loop with a `continue` statement:

```
for (int i=0; i<=5; i++)
```

```
{
    if(i == 3) continue;
    System.out.println("i: "+i)
}
```

A nested for loop with a break and continue statement:

```
for (int i=0; i<=5; i++)
{
    if(i == 3) continue;

    for (int j=0; j<=5; j++)
    {
        if(j == 3) break;
        System.out.println("i: "+i+" j: "+j);
    }
}
```

As you can probably surmise, it's easy to inadvertently introduce bugs when you use some of the preceding code blocks: use them only if it's really necessary to do so, and make sure to test them well.

WORKING WITH WHILE LOOPS

The choice of a for loop versus a while loop depends mainly on your preference; however, sometimes a while loop can be slightly clearer than a for loop (the choice depends on the specific task).

Listing 4.7 displays the content of WhileLoops1.java that iterates through a set of numbers and prints their values.

LISTING 4.7: WhileLoops1.java

```
public class WhileLoops1
{
    private int maxCount1 = 8;
    private double sum1 = 0;

    public WhileLoops1() {}

    public void calculateAverage()
    {
        int i=0;
        while(i<maxCount1)
        {
            sum1 += i;
            System.out.println("Partial sum: "+sum1);
            ++i;
        }

        double avg = sum1/maxCount1;
        System.out.println("Total:    "+sum1);
        System.out.println("Average: "+avg);
    }
```

```
    public static void main(String args[])
    {
        WhileLoops1 wl1 = new WhileLoops1();
        wl1.calculateAverage();
    }
}
```

Listing 4.7 defines the class `WhileLoops1` that contains the method `calculateAverage()` to calculate the sum and the average of a set of numbers. Specifically, the `calculateAverage()` method computes the sum of the integers between 1 and `maxCount1` (the latter has initial value 8) and the average value, which are assigned to the variables `sum1` and `avg`, respectively. Launch the code in Listing 4.7 and you will see the following output:

```
Partial sum: 0.0
Partial sum: 1.0
Partial sum: 3.0
Partial sum: 6.0
Partial sum: 10.0
Partial sum: 15.0
Partial sum: 21.0
Partial sum: 28.0
Total:    28.0
Average: 3.5
```

As a simple exercise, convert the `while` loop in Listing 4.7 to a `for` loop and compare the results.

The next section shows you how to combine `while` loops with conditional logic (if-else statements).

FINDING THE DIVISORS OF A NUMBER

Listing 4.8 displays the content of `Divisors1.java` that contains a `while` loop, conditional logic, and the `%` (modulus) operator to find the prime factors of any integer greater than 1.

LISTING 4.8: Divisors1.java

```
public class Divisors1
{
    public Divisors1() {}

    public void divisors(int num)
    {
        int div = 2;

        System.out.println("Number: "+num);

        while(num > 1)
        {
            if(num % div == 0)
            {
```

```
            System.out.println("divisor: "+div);
            num /= div;
        }
        else
        {
            ++div;
        }
    }
}

public static void main(String args[])
{
    Divisors1 d1 = new Divisors1();
    d1.divisors(12);
}
}
```

Listing 4.8 defines the class `Divisors1` that contains the method `divisors()` that determines the divisors of a positive integer num. The `divisors()` method contains a while loop that iterates while the value of the variable num is greater than 1.

During each iteration, if num is evenly divisible by div, then the value of div is displayed, and then num is reduced by dividing it by the value of div. If num is not evenly divisible by div, then div is incremented by 1. The output from Listing 4.8 is here:

```
Number: 12
divisor: 2
divisor: 2
divisor: 3
```

WORKING WITH DO-WHILE LOOPS

A while loop starts with a conditional statement to determine whether to execute the body of the while loop. A do-while loop executes the body of the loop and *then* checks the conditional statement. Hence, a while loop might not execute (based on whether its conditional statement is true), whereas a do-while loop will *always* execute at least once.

Listing 4.9 displays the content of DoWhile1.java that iterates through a set of numbers and prints their values.

LISTING 4.9: DoWhile1.java

```
public class DoWhile1
{
    private int maxCount1 = 8;

    public DoWhile1() {}

    public void showNumbers()
    {
        int i = maxCount1;
```

```
       do {
           System.out.println("i: "+i);
           i++;
       }
       while(i<maxCount1);
    }

    public static void main(String args[])
    {
       DoWhile1 do1 = new DoWhile1();
       do1.showNumbers();
    }
}
```

Listing 4.9 defines the class DoWhile1 that contains the method showNumbers() whose do-while loop prints the value of a variable i as long as the value of i is less than the value of maxCount1.

Notice that i is initialized with the value of maxCount1, and then the value of i is printed inside the loop, even though it equals maxCount1. This occurs because the conditional logic does not check the value of i until *after* the body of the loop is executed. Launch the code in Listing 4.9 and you will see the following output:

```
i: 8
```

WORKING WITH A JAVA SWITCH STATEMENT

A switch statement is similar to a set of multiple if-else-if statements, but there are some important differences: multiple options in a switch statement can "fall through" to execute the same code block, which can be implemented via multiple "and" statements in the if-else-if style of code.

Listing 4.10 displays the content of Switch1.java that displays a string based on the value of an integer variable month.

LISTING 4.10: Switch1.java

```
public class Switch1
{
    public static void main(String[] args)
    {
       int month = 5;
       String theMonth;

       switch (month) {
       case 0: theMonth = "January";
               break;
       case 1: theMonth = "February";
               break;
       case 2: theMonth = "March";
               break;
       case 3: theMonth = "April";
               break;
```

```
     case 4: theMonth = "May";
             break;
     default: theMonth = "After May";
             break;
     }
     System.out.println("Month: "+theMonth);
   }
}
```

Listing 4.10 defines the class `Switch1` whose `main()` method contains a `switch()` statement that "matches" the value of the integer variable `month` with its corresponding month of the year.

Specifically, the value of 0 is for January, the value of 1 is February, and so forth, until the value of 11, which is associated with the month of December. Launch the code in Listing 4.10 and you will see the following output:

```
Month: after May
```

JAVA ARRAYS

`Java` arrays contain elements that have the same type, which can be primitive types as well as objects. Common operations include `append()` and `remove()`, which enable you to add and remove an element, respectively. Here are some array operations and properties:

- initializing
- iterating
- length
- single/multidimensional
- sorting
- varargs
- ArrayIndexOutOfBoundsException

Listing 4.11 displays the content of `SimpleArray.java` that illustrates how to perform simple array operations.

LISTING 4.11: SimpleArray.java

```
import java.lang.ArrayIndexOutOfBoundsException;

public class SimpleArray
{
   public SimpleArray() {}

   public static void main(String args[])
   {
      int index = 5;
      int[] numbers = {3, 5, 19, -123};
      System.out.println("length: " +numbers.length);

      System.out.print("numbers: ");
```

```
for(int num : numbers)
{
    System.out.print(num+" ");
}
System.out.println("");

try {
    System.out.print("index "+index+": "+
    numbers[index]);
} catch(ArrayIndexOutOfBoundsException aioob) {
    System.out.println("Index "+index+" exceeds
    "+numbers.length);
}
    }
}
```

Listing 4.11 defines the class `SimpleArray` and a `main()` method that initializes the numeric array `numbers` with four numbers. The next portion of the `main()` method contains a `for` loop that displays the content of the `numbers` array.

The final portion of the `main()` method contains a `try/catch` code block in which the code attempts to access an element beyond the last element in the `numbers` array. In addition, the final code block throws an exception that is handled in the `catch` block. Launch the code in Listing 4.11 and you will see the following output:

```
length: 4
numbers: 3 5 19 -123
Index 5 exceeds 4
```

WORKING WITH ARRAYS OF NUMBERS

`Java` arrays contain elements that have the same type, which can be primitive values or objects (which must be of the same type). One way to create a `Java` array is to declare an array variable and also initialize the array in the same line of code. Here is an example:

```
private String[] letters = {"a", "b", "c"};
```

Another way involves declaring an array variable and then using a loop to populate the elements of the array variable:

1. Declare a variable to hold the array values.
2. Create a new array object and assign it to an element in the array variable.
3. Repeat Step 2 until the array is full.

The following code snippets declare arrays whose elements are of type `String`, `double`, `int`, and `MyClass`, respectively:

- `String wordlist[];`
- `double prices[];`
- `int intValues[];`
- `MyClass myClasses[];`

An alternate and equivalent approach that is used in this book is shown here:

- `String[] wordList;`
- `double[] prices;`
- `int[] intValues;`
- `MyClass[] myClasses;`

Listing 4.12 displays the content of `Arrays1.java` that illustrates how to declare arrays and then initialize the elements of the arrays.

LISTING 4.12: Arrays1.java

```
public class Arrays1
{
   private int arraySize = 12;
   private double intSum = 0;
   private double intAvg = 0;
   private double dblSum = 0.0;
   private double dblAvg = 0.0;

   double[] prices = new double[arraySize];
   int[] intValues = new int[arraySize];
   private String[] letters = {"a", "b", "c"};

   public Arrays1() {}

   public void initializeValues()
   {
      for(int i=0; i<arraySize; i++)
      {
         prices[i]    = 20.0*Math.random();
         intValues[i] = (int)(40*Math.random());
      }
   }

   public void calculateAverage()
   {
      for(int i=0; i<arraySize; i++)
      {
         intSum += intValues[i];
         dblSum += prices[i];
      }

      double dblAvg = dblSum/arraySize;
      int intAvg = (int)(intSum/arraySize);

      System.out.println("Total Price:     "+dblSum);
      System.out.println("Avg Price:       "+dblAvg);
      System.out.println("Total intValues: "+intSum);
      System.out.println("Avg intValues:   "+intAvg);
      System.out.println();

      for(int i=0; i<letters.length; i++)
```

```
        {
            System.out.println("Letter "+(i+1)+":
            "+letters[i]);
        }
    }

    public static void main(String args[])
    {
        Arrays1 arr1 = new Arrays1();
        arr1.initializeValues();
        arr1.calculateAverage();
    }
}
```

Listing 4.12 defines the class `Arrays1` that contains the methods `initializeValues()` to initialize the elements of the `prices` array with randomly generated decimal numbers and also initialize the elements of the `intValues` array with randomly generated positive integers.

Listing 4.12 also defines the method `calculateAverage()` that calculates the average of the integer values and the average of the decimal values in the arrays `intValues` and `prices`, respectively. After displaying the total sum and the average sum, the method `calculateAverage()` contains a loop that iterates through the elements of the string array `letters`. The output from Listing 4.12 is here:

```
Total Price:        114.57135984015864
Avg Price:          9.54761332001322
Total intValues:    232.0
Avg intValues:      19

Letter 1: a
Letter 2: b
Letter 3: c
```

THE BUBBLE SORT ALGORITHM

The bubble sort is a well-known sorting algorithm. Listing 4.13 displays the content of `BubbleSort.java` that illustrates how to sort an array of numbers in increasing order.

LISTING 4.13: BubbleSort.java

```
public class BubbleSort
{
    public BubbleSort() {}

    public void sortNumbers()
    {
        int[] numbers = {-3, 50, 10, 5, 20, 300, -200};

        System.out.println("Original array:");
        for(int i=0; i<numbers.length; i++)
```

```
    {
        System.out.print(numbers[i]+" ");
    }
    System.out.println();

    for(int i=0; i<numbers.length-1; i++)
    {
        for(int j=i+1; j<numbers.length; j++)
        {
            if(numbers[i] > numbers[j])
            {
                int temp = numbers[i];
                numbers[i] = numbers[j];
                numbers[j] = temp;
            }
        }
    }

    System.out.println("Sorted array:");
    for(int i=0; i<numbers.length; i++)
    {
        System.out.print(numbers[i]+" ");
    }
    System.out.println();
    }
    public static void main(String args[])
    {
        BubbleSort bs = new BubbleSort();
        bs.sortNumbers();
    }
}
```

Listing 4.13 defines the class BubbleSort with a main() method that initializes the variable bs as an instance of the BubbleSort class, and then invokes the method sortNumbers().

This method contains a nested loop that iterates through the elements of the array numbers that contains integer values. Given an index position i, the code examines the contents of the index positions that are greater than i. If one of those index positions (let's call it position j) contains an array value that is greater than the array value at index i, then the array elements numbers[i] and numbers[j] are switched (using the integer value temp as a temporary value). Launch the code in Listing 4.13 and you will see the following output:

```
Original array:
-3 50 10 5 20 300 -200
Sorted array:
-200 -3 5 10 20 50 300
```

JAVA MULTI-DIMENSIONAL ARRAYS

In addition to one-dimensional arrays, Java also supports multi-dimensional arrays. Listing 4.14 displays the content of MultiDimArrays1.java that illustrates how to initialize a two-dimensional array.

LISTING 4.14: MultiDimArrays1.java

```java
public class MultiDimArrays1
{
    private int rowCount    = 4;
    private int colCount    = 4;
    private double dblSum = 0.0;
    private double dblAvg = 0.0;

    double[][] myMatrix = new double[rowCount][colCount];

    public MultiDimArrays1() {}

    public void initializeValues()
    {
        for(int row=0; row<rowCount; row++) {
            for(int col=0; col<colCount; col++) {
                myMatrix[row][col] = 5.0*(row+col);
            }
        }
    }

    public void calculateAverage()
    {
        // calculate sum and display values
        for(int row=0; row<rowCount; row++) {
            for(int col=0; col<colCount; col++) {
                dblSum += myMatrix[row][col];

                System.out.println("("+row+","+col+"): "+
                myMatrix[row][col]);
            }
            System.out.println();
        }

        double dblAvg = dblSum/(rowCount*colCount);
        System.out.println("Total Sum: "+dblSum);
        System.out.println("Avg Value: "+dblAvg);
    }

    public static void main(String args[])
    {
        MultiDimArrays1 arr1 = new MultiDimArrays1();
        arr1.initializeValues();
        arr1.calculateAverage();
    }
}
```

Listing 4.14 defines the class `MultiDimArrays1` with the methods `initializeValues()` and `calculateAverage()`, both of which are similar to Listing 4.12.

The new code involves a nested loop that iterates through the elements of the two-dimensional array `myMatrix` of decimal values. The outer loop iterates through the rows of `myMatrix`, and the inner loop calculates the sum of the values in the current row. Thus, the nested loop calculates the row-oriented sum of the decimal values in `myMatrix`.

The output from Listing 4.14 is here:

```
(0,0): 0.0
(0,1): 5.0
(0,2): 10.0
(0,3): 15.0

(1,0): 5.0
(1,1): 10.0
(1,2): 15.0
(1,3): 20.0

(2,0): 10.0
(2,1): 15.0
(2,2): 20.0
(2,3): 25.0

(3,0): 15.0
(3,1): 20.0
(3,2): 25.0
(3,3): 30.0

Total Sum: 240.0
Avg Value: 15.0
```

JAVA MULTI-DIMENSIONAL ARRAYS (2)

Listing 4.15 displays the content of MultiDimArrays2.java that illustrates how to initialize a two-dimensional array and a three-dimensional array.

LISTING 4.15: MultiDimArrays2.java

```java
public class MultiDimArrays2
{
    public MultiDimArrays2() {}

    public void Array1D()
    {
        // Declare/initialize a 1D array:
        int arr1[] = {1,2,3,4,5,6,7,8,9};

        System.out.println("Contents of 1D array:");
        for(int i=0; i<9; i++)
        {
            System.out.print(arr1[i] + " ");
        }
        System.out.println();
    }

    public void Array2D()
    {
        // Declare/initialize a 2D array:
        int arr2[][] = {{1,2,3}, {4,5,6}, {7,8,9}};

        System.out.println("Contents of 2D array:");
        for(int i=0; i<3; i++)
```

```java
        {
            for(int j=0; j<3; j++)
            {
                System.out.print(arr2[i][j] + " ");
            }
            System.out.println();
        }
    }

    public void Array3D()
    {
        // Declare/initialize a 3D array:
        int arr3[][][] = {{{1,2,3}, {4,5,6}, {7,8,9}},
                          {{11,12,13}, {14,15,16}, {17,18,19}},
                          {{21,22,23}, {24,25,26}, {27,28,29}}};
        System.out.println("Contents of 3D array:");
        for(int i=0; i<3; i++)
        {
            for(int j=0; j<3; j++)
            {
                for(int k=0; k<3; k++)
                {
                    System.out.print(arr3[i][j][k] + " ");
                }
                System.out.println();
            }
            System.out.println();
        }
    }

    public static void main(String args[])
    {
        MultiDimArrays2 mda2 = new MultiDimArrays2();

        mda2.Array1D();
        mda2.Array2D();
        mda2.Array3D();
    }
}
```

Listing 4.15 defines the class `MultiDimArrays2` and a `main()` method that initializes the variable `mda2` as an instance of the `MultiDimArrays2` class. Next, the method `Array1D()` defines and initializes a one-dimensional array, followed by a loop that prints the values of that array.

Next, the method `Array2D()` defines and initializes a two-dimensional array, followed by a nested loop that prints the values of that array.

Similarly, the `Array3D()` method defines and initializes a three-dimensional array, followed by a triple-nested loop that prints the values of that array. The output from Listing 4.15 is here:

```
Contents of 1D array:
1 2 3 4 5 6 7 8 9
Contents of 2D array:
1 2 3
4 5 6
7 8 9
```

```
Contents of 3D array:
1 2 3
4 5 6
7 8 9

11 12 13
14 15 16
17 18 19

21 22 23
24 25 26
27 28 29
```

WORKING WITH CHARACTERS AND STRINGS

Listing 4.16 displays the content of DisplayChars1.java that illustrates how to print the characters in a text string, along with information about each character (digit, uppercase, lowercase, or space).

LISTING 4.16: DisplayChars1.java

```java
public class DisplayChars1
{
    public static void main(String args[])
    {
        char chr, upr, lwr;
        String line  = "Some 5text";
        String lower = line.toLowerCase();
        String upper = line.toUpperCase();

        System.out.println("Line:   "+line);
        System.out.println("Length: "+line.length()+"\n");

        for(int i=0; i<line.length(); i++)
        {
            chr = line.charAt(i);
            lwr = lower.charAt(i);
            upr = upper.charAt(i);

            if(chr == ' ') {
                System.out.println("Position "+i+":
                [Space]");
            }
            else if(Character.isDigit(chr)) {
                System.out.println("Position "+i+": "+line.
                charAt(i)+" [DIGIT]");
            }
            else if(chr == lwr) {
                System.out.println("Position "+i+": "+line.
                charAt(i)+" [lowercase]");
            }
            else if(chr == upr) {
                System.out.println("Position "+i+": "+line.
                charAt(i)+" [UPPERCASE]");
            }
```

```
        else
        {
            System.out.println("Position "+i+":  "+line.
            charAt(i));
        }
    }
  }
}
```

Listing 4.16 defines the class `DisplayChars1` whose `main()` method contains a `for` loop that iterates through the characters in the variable `line` that is initialized as the text string `"Some 5text"`. The variable `chr` holds the character at index `i` of the variable `line`, whereas `lwr` and `upr` are the lowercase and uppercase letters, respectively, of the letter in `chr`.

The loop contains conditional logic that first checks if `chr` is a blank space, followed by a code block to check if `chr` is a digit by means of the method `Character.isDigit()`. The remaining conditional blocks compare `chr` with `lwr` and `upr` to check if `chr` is an uppercase letter or lowercase letter. Launch the code in Listing 4.16 and you will see the following output:

```
Line:    Some 5text
Length: 10

Position 0: S [UPPERCASE]
Position 1: o [lowercase]
Position 2: m [lowercase]
Position 3: e [lowercase]
Position 4:   [Space]
Position 5: 5 [DIGIT]
Position 6: t [lowercase]
Position 7: e [lowercase]
Position 8: x [lowercase]
Position 9: t [lowercase]
```

As you can see, the code in Listing 4.16 does not check for punctuation and special characters such as ":," "#," or "[."

WORKING WITH ARRAYS OF STRINGS

This section shows you how to print the names of people from the `main()` method, where the first names and last names are stored in arrays.

Listing 4.17 displays the content of `PersonArray.java` that contains two private `String` variables for keeping track of a person's first name and last name, along with methods that enable you to access the first name and last name of any person.

LISTING 4.17: PersonArray.java

```
public class PersonArray
{
    private String[] firstNames = {"Jane","John","Bob"};
    private String[] lastNames  = {"Smith","Jones","Stone"};
```

```
public void displayNames()
{
   for(int i=0; i<firstNames.length; i++)
   {
      System.out.println("My name is "+
                         firstNames[i]+" "+
                         lastNames[i]);
   }
}
public static void main (String args[])
{
   PersonArray pa = new PersonArray();
   pa.displayNames();
}
}
```

Listing 4.17 defines the class `PersonArray` that contains the method `displayNames()` whose `for` loop iterates through the string arrays `firstNames` and `lastNames`. The loop variable `i` is used as an index into these arrays to print a person's first name and last name, as shown here:

```
System.out.println("My name is "+
                   firstNames[i]+" "+
                   lastNames[i]);
```

Launch the code in Listing 4.17 and you will see the following output:

```
My name is John Smith
My name is Jane Andrews
```

DISPLAYING COMMAND LINE ARGUMENTS

Listing 4.18 displays the content of `CommandLineArgs.java` that illustrates how to display the command line arguments that have been supplied to a class.

LISTING 4.18: CommandLineArgs.java

```
import java.lang.NumberFormatException;

public class CommandLineArgs
{
   public static void main(String[] args)
   {
      String msg = "";

      for(int i=0; i<args.length; i++)
      {
         try {
            int t = Integer.parseInt(args[i]);
            msg = ": Integer: YES";
         } catch (NumberFormatException nfe) {
            msg = ": Integer: NO";
         }
```

```
        System.out.println("args["+i+"]: "+args[i]+msg);
    }

  }
}
```

Listing 4.18 defines the class `CommandLineArgs` that contains a `main()` method with a `for` loop that iterates through each string that was specified on the command line.

During each iteration, a `try/catch` block contains some code to determine whether the current command line argument is an integer, after which a corresponding message is displayed for that command line argument. Launch the code in Listing 4.18 as shown here:

```
java CommandLineArgs a b 1 2 c d
```

The preceding invocation of `CommandLineArgs` will display the following output:

```
args[0]: a: Integer: NO
args[1]: b: Integer: NO
args[2]: 1: Integer: YES
args[3]: 2: Integer: YES
args[4]: c: Integer: NO
args[5]: d: Integer: NO
```

RANDOMLY ACCESSING ARRAYS OF STRINGS

This section shows you how to print the names of people from the `main()` method, where the first names and last names are stored in arrays.

Listing 4.19 displays the content of `PersonRandom.java` that uses a randomly generated index into an array of names in order to print a person's first name and last name.

LISTING 4.19: PersonRandom.java

```
public class PersonRandom
{
    private String[] firstNames = {"Jane", "John", "Bob"};
    private String[] lastNames  = {"Smith", "Jones",
"Stone"};

    public void displayNames()
    {
        String fname, lname;
        int index, loopCount=6, maxRange=20;
        int pCount = firstNames.length;

        for(int i=0; i<loopCount; i++)
        {
            index = (int)(maxRange*Math.random());
            index = index % pCount;

            fname = firstNames[index];
```

```
        lname = lastNames[index];

        System.out.println("My name is "+
                           fname+" "+lname);
    }
}
public static void main (String args[])
{
    PersonRandom pa = new PersonRandom();
    pa.displayNames();
}
}
```

Listing 4.19 is very similar to the code in Listing 4.16: the important difference is that a name is chosen by means of a randomly generated number, as shown here:

```
index = (int)(maxRange*Math.random());
```

Launch the code in Listing 4.19 and you will see the following output:

```
My name is Jane Smith
My name is John Jones
My name is Jane Smith
My name is Jane Smith
My name is Bob Stone
My name is John Jones
```

Notice that there are 6 output lines even though there are only 3 people. This is possible because the randomly generated number is always between 0 and 2, which means that we can generate hundreds of lines of output. Of course, there will be many duplicate output lines because there are only 3 distinct people.

THE STRINGBUILDER AND STRINGBUFFER CLASSES

Recall that the `String` class creates an immutable sequence of characters, which can involve a significant amount of memory for many large strings. The `StringBuilder` class is an alternative to the `String` class that supports a mutable sequence of characters.

The `StringBuilder` class has a number of useful methods, each of which has return type `StringBuilder`, as shown below:

- `capacity()`
- `charAt()`
- `delete()`
- `codePointAt()`
- `codePointBefore()`
- `codePointCount()`
- `deleteCharAt()`
- `ensureCapacity()`

- getChars()
- length()
- replace()
- reverse()
- setCharAt()
- setLength()
- subSequence()

The StringBuffer class is similar to the StringBuilder class. Although both of them provide an alternative to the String class by making a mutable sequence of characters, they have different behavior in terms of synchronization.

The StringBuilder class is *not* thread-safe, whereas the StringBuffer class guarantees synchronization. Hence, if you need thread-safe code, use the StringBuffer class; if your code has a single thread, use the StringBuilder class because it will be faster in most situations.

Java Example with StringBuilder and StringBuffer Classes

Listing 4.20 displays the content of ReverseString.java that reverses a string using the StringBuilder class as well as the StringBuffer class.

LISTING 4.20: ReverseString.java

```
public class ReverseString
{
    private int maxCount1 = 8;
    private double sum1 = 0;

    public ReverseString() {}

    public void reverse1(String str)
    {
        System.out.println("Original:  "+str);

        int strLength = str.length();
        char[] strArray = str.toCharArray();
        for(int i=0; i<strLength/2; i++)
        {
            char temp = strArray[i];
            strArray[i] = strArray[strLength-1-i];
            strArray[strLength-1-i] = temp;
        }
        System.out.println("Reversed1: "+String.
        valueOf(strArray));

        strArray = new char[str.length()];
        for(int i=0; i<strLength/2; i++)
        {
            char temp = str.charAt(i);
            strArray[i] = str.charAt(strLength-1-i);
            strArray[strLength-1-i] = temp;
        }
```

```
        System.out.println("Reversed1: "+String.
        valueOf(strArray));
    }
    public void reverse2(String str)
    {
        String reversed = "";
        for(int i=str.length()-1; i>=0; i--)
        {
            reversed += str.charAt(i);
        }
        System.out.println("Reversed2: "+reversed);
    }
    public void reverse3(String str)
    {
        StringBuffer reversed = new StringBuffer(str);
        System.out.println("Reversed3: "+reversed.reverse());
    }
    public void reverse4(String str)
    {
        StringBuilder reversed = new StringBuilder();
        for(int i=str.length()-1; i>=0; i--)
        {
            reversed.append(str.charAt(i));
        }
        System.out.println("Reversed4: "+reversed);
    }
    public static void main(String args[])
    {
        ReverseString rs = new ReverseString();
        rs.reverse1("abcd");
        rs.reverse2("abcd");
        rs.reverse3("abcd");
        rs.reverse4("abcd");
    }
}
```

Listing 4.20 defines the class ReverseString that contains four methods that can reverse a string. The method reverse1() contains two loops that use a temporary variable to swap the elements of an array of characters, starting from the left-most and right-most character pair, and moving inward toward the midpoint of the array. The first loop switches the characters in the character-based variable strArray, whereas the second array works with the strArray that is initialized large enough to hold the characters in the string variable str that is a parameter of this method.

The method reverse2() contains a loop that works in reverse order to append the characters of the parameter str in a right-to-left fashion (using the += operator) to the string variable reversed, after which this variable will contain the characters of str in reverse order.

The method reverse3() invokes the reverse() method to reverse the contents of the parameter str.

The method `reverse4()` is similar to `reverse2()`, except that it uses the `append()` method to concatenate characters to the string reversed instead of the += operator.

The `main()` method initializes the variable `rs` as an instance of the `ReverseString` class, and then invokes each of the four preceding methods to reverse the contents of a string.

Launch the code in Listing 4.20 and you will see the following output:

```
dcba
dcba
dcba
dcba
```

The next section delves into recursion, which is a powerful technique for solving a myriad of tasks, such as calculating factorial values and computing Fibonacci numbers.

WHAT IS RECURSION?

Recursion is an elegant and powerful technique for solving tasks, yet it can also be confusing if you are new to recursion. In brief, a recursive function is a function that is defined in terms of itself. While this might see odd, it's actually a convenient way to express some formulas and to solve tasks that would be cumbersome to solve using iterative algorithms.

Later you will see complete code samples that illustrate how to use recursion to calculate some well-known values. Although you probably won't need all of them in your own work, they will provide you with useful reinforcement regarding recursion.

For instance, the factorial function `f(n)` is the product of all the integers between 1 and n. For simplicity, let's assume that n is a positive integer in order to make the code simpler. This means that `f(1) = 1, f(2) = 2, f(3) = 6, f(4) = 24`, and so on. In fact, according to the definition of factorial,

```
f(n) = 1*2*3 . . . * n.
```

The preceding is an iterative definition, whereas this is the recursive definition:

```
f(n) = n*f(n-1) for n > 0 and f(0) = 1.
```

Note: Any recursive function has a "closed form" (non-recursive) equivalent representation and vice versa.

The following subsections contain examples of recursive definitions of functions and their iterative counterparts for computing some well-known values.

Adding Integers

The recursive definition of the sum of the first n positive integers is here:

```
recursive(1) = 1;
recursive(n) = n+recursive(n-1);
```

The recursive definition for the preceding function is shown here:

```
if(n <= 1) { return 1; }
else       { return n+recursive (n-1); }
```

The iterative code for the preceding function is shown here:

```
int sum = 0;
for(int i=1; i<=n; i++) {
  sum += i;
}
```

Instead of invoking the preceding code, you can use the closed form solution for the sum of the integer from 1 to n: `sum = n*(n-1)/2`.

Powers of Two

The recursive definition for calculating powers of 2 is here:

```
recursive(0) = 1;
recursive(n) = 2*recursive(n-1);
```

The recursive code for the preceding function is shown here:

```
if(n== 0) { return 1; }
else      { return 2*prod(n-1); }
```

The iterative code for the preceding function is shown here:

```
int prod = 1;
for(int i=1; i<=n; i++) {
  prod *= i;
}
```

Instead of invoking the preceding code, you can use the closed form solution for the sum of the integer from 1 to n: `sum = 2^n`.

Factorial Values

The recursive definition of the product of the first n positive integers is here:

```
factorial(1) = 1;
factorial(n) = n*factorial(n-1);
```

The recursive code for the preceding function is shown here:

```
if(n <= 1) { return 1; }
else       { return n*factorial(n-1); }
```

The iterative code for the preceding function is shown here:

```
int factorial = 1;
for(int i=1; i<=n; i++) {
  factorial *= i;
}
```

Instead of invoking the preceding code, you can use the closed form solution for the product of the integers from 1 to n: `factorial(n)` = `n*(n-1)*(n-2)....3*2*1`

Fibonacci Numbers

The recursive definition of Fibonacci numbers is here:

```
fib(0) = 0;
fib(1) = 1;
fib(n) = fib(n-1)+fib(n-2);
```

The recursive code for the preceding function is shown here:

```
if(n <= 1) { return 1; }
else       { return n*factorial(n-1); }
```

CALCULATING FACTORIAL VALUES

As you have seen, the factorial value of a positive integer n is the product of all the integers between 1 and n. The symbol for factorial is the exclamation point (!) and some sample factorial values are here:

```
1! = 1
2! = 2
3! = 6
4! = 20
5! = 120
```

Listing 4.21 displays the content of `Factorial.java` that illustrates how to use recursion to calculate the factorial value of a positive integer.

LISTING 4.21: Factorial.java

```
public class Factorial
{
    public Factorial() {}

    public int factorial(int num)
    {
        if(num > 1)
        {
            return num * factorial(num-1);
        }
```

```
        else
        {
            return 1;
        }
    }

    public static void main(String args[])
    {
        Factorial f1 = new Factorial();
        int result = f1.factorial(5);
        System.out.println("The factorial of 5 = "+result);
    }
}
```

Listing 4.21 contains the function `factorial` that implements the recursive definition of the factorial value of a number. The output from Listing 4.21 is here:

```
The factorial of 5 = 120
```

In addition to a recursive solution, there is also an iterative solution for calculating the factorial value of a number.

Listing 4.22 displays the content of `Factorial2.java` that illustrates how to use a `for` loop to calculate the factorial value of a positive integer.

LISTING 4.22: Factorial2.java

```
public class Factorial2
{
    public Factorial2() {}

    public int factorial(int num)
    {
        int prod = 1;

        for(int i=2; i<num+1; i++)
        {
            prod *= i;
        }

        return prod;
    }

    public static void main(String args[])
    {
        Factorial2 f2 = new Factorial2();
        int result = f2.factorial(5);
        System.out.println("The factorial of 5 = "+result);
    }
}
```

Listing 4.22 defines the function `factorial2()` with a parameter `num`, followed by the variable `prod` that has an initial value of 1. The next part of `factorial2` is a `for` loop whose loop variable `i` ranges between 2 and `num+1`, and each iteration through that loop multiples the value of `prod` with the value of i, thereby computing the factorial value of num. The output from Listing 4.22 is here:

```
The factorial of 5 = 120
```

CALCULATING THE GCD OF TWO NUMBERS

The GCD (greatest common divisor) of two positive integers is the largest integer that divides both integers with a remainder of 0. Some values are shown here:

```
gcd(6,2)   = 2
gcd(10,4)  = 2
gcd(24,16) = 8
```

Listing 4.23 uses recursion and Euclid's algorithm in order to find the GCD of two positive integers. Although it's possible to make the code more compact, this version of the algorithm makes the logic clearer.

LISTING 4.23: GCD.java

```java
public class GCD
{
    public GCD() {}

    public int gcd(int num1, int num2)
    {
        if(num1 % num2 == 0) {
            return num2;
        }
        else if (num1 < num2) {
            System.out.println("Switching "+num1+" and
            "+num2);
            return gcd(num2, num1);
        }
        else {
            System.out.println("Reducing "+num1+" and
            "+num2);
            return gcd(num1-num2, num2);
        }
    }

    public static void main(String args[])
    {
        GCD g = new GCD();
        int result = g.gcd(24,10);
        System.out.println("The GCD of 24 and 10 =
        "+result);
    }
}
```

Listing 4.23 defines the function gcd() with the parameters num1 and num2. If num1 is divisible by num2, the function returns num2. If num1 is less than num2, then gcd() is invoked by switching the order of num1 and num2. In all other cases, gcd() returns the result of computing gcd() with the values num1−num2 and num2. The output from Listing 4.23 is here:

```
Reducing 24 and 10
Reducing 14 and 10
Switching 4 and 10
Reducing 10 and 4
Reducing 6 and 4
Switching 2 and 4
The GCD of 24 and 10 = 2
```

COUNTING DIGITS IN INTEGERS

Listing 4.24 uses recursion to find the number of digits in a positive integer. For example, the number 99 has two digits, the number 3821 has four digits, and so forth.

LISTING 4.24: CountDigits.java

```java
public class CountingDigits
{
    public CountDigits() {}

    public int countDigits(int num, int result)
    {
        if( num == 0 )
        {
            return result;
        }
        else
        {
            return countDigits(num/10, result+1);
        }
    }

    public static void main(String args[])
    {
        CountDigits cd = new CountDigits();

        int number = 123, result = 0;
        int[] numbers  = {1234, 767, 1234321, -101};

        result = cd.countDigits(number, 0);
        System.out.println("Digits in "+number+" = "+result);

        for (int num : numbers)
        {
            result = cd.countDigits(num, 0);
            System.out.println("Digits in "+num+" = "+result);
        }
    }
}
```

Listing 4.24 defines the class `CountDigits` that contains the method `countDigits()` that counts the number of digits in the number assigned to the variable num. Note that this function is recursive: the terminating condition occurs when num is 0, in which case the value of `result` is returned. Otherwise, the function `countDigits()` is invoked by passing the value num/10 as the new number, and also passing the value `result+1` (because we have counted another digit).

Next, the `main()` method creates an instance cd of the `countDigits` class and initializes the array numbers of integers. The final portion of Listing 4.24 is a loop that invokes the `countDigits()` method with each number in the numbers array. The output from Listing 4.24 is here:

```
Digits in 123 = 3
Digits in 1234 = 4
Digits in 767 = 3
Digits in 1234321 = 7
Digits in -101 = 3
```

One other interesting point is that the code in Listing 4.24 works correctly for both positive and negative integers.

ADDING DIGITS IN INTEGERS

Listing 4.25 uses recursion to find the sum of the digits in an integer. For example, the number 99 has a sum of 18, the number 3821 has a sum of 14, and so forth.

LISTING 4.25: AddDigits.java

```java
public class AddDigits
{
    public AddDigits() {}

    // recursive solution
    public int computeSum(int num, int result)
    {
        if( num == 0 )
        {
            return result;
        }
        else
        {
            return computeSum(num/10, result + num % 10);
        }
    }

    // iterative solution
    public int simpleSum(int num)
    {
        int sum = 0;
```

```
        while (num > 0)
        {
            sum += num % 10;
            num /= 10;
        }

        return sum;
    }

    public static void main(String args[])
    {
        int result = 0;
        int[] numbers  = {1234, 767, 1234321, -101};

        AddDigits cd = new AddDigits();

        for (int num : numbers)
        {
            result = cd.computeSum(num, 0);
            System.out.println("1Digit sum in "+num+" =
            "+result);
            result = cd.simpleSum(num);
            System.out.println("2Digit sum in "+num+" =
            "+result);
        }
    }
}
```

Listing 4.25 defines the class AddDigits that contains the method computeSum() that uses recursion to count the number of digits in the number assigned to the variable num. Note that this function is recursive: the terminating condition occurs when num is 0, in which case the value of result is returned. Otherwise, the function countDigits() is invoked by passing the value num/10 as the new number, and also passing the value result+1 (because we have counted another digit).

The other method is simpleSum(), which uses an iterative solution to compute the sum of the digits of a number.

Next, the main() method creates an instance cd of the AddDigits class and initializes the array numbers of integers. The final portion of Listing 4.25 is a loop that invokes the addDigits() method with each number in the numbers array. The output from Listing 4.25 is here:

```
1Digit sum in 1234 = 10
2Digit sum in 1234 = 10
1Digit sum in 767 = 20
2Digit sum in 767 = 20
1Digit sum in 1234321 = 16
2Digit sum in 1234321 = 16
1Digit sum in -101 = -2
2Digit sum in -101 = 0
```

One other interesting point is that the code in Listing 4.24 works differently for positive and negative integers.

REVERSE A STRING VIA RECURSION

Listing 4.26 displays the content of `Reverser.java` that uses recursion to reverse a string using recursion. Chapter 1 shows you a non-recursive example of reversing a string that's simpler than using recursion. This code sample is just for illustrative purposes.

LISTING 4.26: Reverser.java

```java
public class Reverser
{
    public Reverser() {}

    private String reverser(String original)
    {
        if(original.isEmpty())     {
           return original;
        }

        return reverser(original.substring(1))+original.
        charAt(0);
    }

    public static void main(String args[])
    {
        String result;
        String[] names = {"Sally", "Steve", "Robert"};

        Reverser rev = new Reverser();
        for ( String name : names)
        {
            result = rev.reverser(name)
            System.out.println("Word: "+name+" reverse:
            "+result);
        }
    }
}
```

Listing 4.26 defines the class `Reverser` and a `main()` method that initializes the variable `rev` as an instance of the `Reverser` class. A `for` loop iterates through the strings in the `names` array, and then invokes the `reverser()` method that reverses the current string. Launch the code in Listing 4.26 and you will see the following output:

```
Word: Sally reverse: yllaS
Word: Steve reverse: evetS
Word: Robert reverse: treboR
```

SUMMARY

This chapter started with `Java` code samples with `for` loops and `while` loops that contain conditional logic that was introduced in Chapter 1. You learned how to determine whether an integer is even or odd, and whether a given year is a leap year. Next you learned how to work with arrays of strings and numbers.

You also learned about recursion and how to define methods that are invoked recursively in order to calculate the factorial value of a number. You also used recursion to find the prime divisors of a positive integer, as well as the GCD of any pair of positive integers. Finally, you learned how to use recursion to reverse a string.

CHAPTER 5

INTRODUCTION TO OOP

This chapter contains various examples of custom Java classes and introduces various Object-Oriented Programming (OOP) concepts, such as inheritance, encapsulation, and polymorphism. Previous chapters do have a sprinkling of code samples involving OO concepts, intended as a preview of OOP. This chapter provides a consolidated discussion of OOP concepts and Java code samples.

Incidentally, if you are familiar with OOP from working in another programming language, it might be sufficient to simply skim through this chapter, thereby ensuring that you feel comfortable with all the code samples. As a second benefit, you can create a list of the nuances in the Java code samples. Even better, you can convert your existing code samples to Java that will accelerate your learning process.

However, if you are a neophyte, you might need to spend more time to thoroughly grasp the more subtle aspects of OOP concepts and how they are implemented in Java code. To facilitate the learning process, this chapter alternates between concepts and code samples. Furthermore, please read Chapter 2 (if you have not already done so) because the material in this chapter assumes that you are comfortable with the concepts and the code samples in that chapter.

The first part of this chapter shows you how to override a method in a Java class, followed by an explanation of the Java keywords `private`, `protected`, and `public` for variables and methods. The second part of this chapter contains an introduction to inheritance via a code sample, along with value objects that can simplify the testing process and also increase the reusability of your custom classes.

The third part of this chapter discusses inheritance, along with examples of how to instantiate classes with different custom classes. You will also learn about interfaces and abstract classes. The fourth part of this chapter delves into polymorphism, with code samples that illustrate some of the subtler details regarding polymorphism.

JAVA CONSTRUCTORS

You previously learned that a Java class can be viewed informally as a group of functions and data that are called *methods* and *properties (or attributes)*, respectively, whose accessibility is determined via specific keywords. An *instance* of a class is a concrete object, which is to say that it resides somewhere in memory. An instance also has an identity that distinguishes it from other instances of the same class.

Multiple instances of the same class typically have different values for their properties (later you will learn about an exception to this rule). In a subsequent section, you will see that two distinct instances of a class can contain the same content, even though they occupy different memory locations.

The *constructor* in a class enables you to initialize the properties of an instance of a class. In fact, Java enables you to define multiple constructors having different parameters. Listing 5.1 displays the content of MyClass. java that defines two constructors: one is an empty constructor and the other constructor takes two parameters.

LISTING 5.1: MyClass.java

```
public class MyClass
{
    private String fname = "";
    private String lname = "";

    // public empty constructor
    public MyClass()
    {
        //this.MyClass("unknown", "person");
        this("unknown", "person");
    }

    // public constructor
    public MyClass(String fname, String lname)
    {
        this.fname = fname;
        this.lname = lname;
    }

    public static void main(String[] args)
    {
        MyClass inst1 = new MyClass("Dave", "Smith");
        MyClass inst2 = new MyClass();
    }
}
```

Listing 5.1 defines the class MyClass and the main() method initializes the variables inst1 and inst2 as instances of MyClass. Notice that inst1 is created by invoking the constructor that takes two parameters, whereas `inst2` is created by invoking the empty constructor.

As a reminder, in Chapter 3 you learned that a constructor in a class can be invoked in several ways, as shown in the following list:

1. Using new keyword (constructor is invoked)
2. Using the `newInstance()` method of the Class class (constructor is invoked)
3. Using the `newInstance()` method of the Constructor class (constructor is invoked)
4. Using the `clone()` method (no constructor call)
5. Using deserialization (no constructor call)

Overloading Java Methods

In addition to overriding a method, `Java` allows you to *overload* the name of a method; however, the arguments of the two methods must differ in number or in type (or both). The *signature* of a method is the combination of the data types of the arguments of the method. Some examples are listed below:

```
public void add(int x1, int x2)            { ... }
public void add(int x1, double x2)          { ... }
public void add(int x1, int x2, int x3)     { ... }
```

The preceding methods have the following signatures added to the method name:

```
int,int
int,double
int,int,int
```

Overloading methods enables your class to support a wider range of data types. This is true for "regular" methods, as well as the constructor of a `Java` class. As a trivial example, you can define an `add()` method that adds two numbers, and also define an `add()` method that "adds" two strings by concatenating them. The only difference is the signature: `add(int, int)` for adding integers and `add(String, String)` for adding strings.

Note that *overriding* a method is a different concept: this occurs when class A is a subclass of class B, and both classes have a method *with the same name and signature*. This scenario is described in more detail later in this chapter in the section that discusses inheritance. However, before we delve into inheritance, we need to look at some keywords that control the visibility of variables and methods, which is the topic of the next section.

PUBLIC, PROTECTED, AND PRIVATE KEYWORDS

Recall that Chapter 3 discussed these `Java` keywords, along with some code snippets, whereas this section contains a complete code sample.

Listing 5.2 displays the content of ClassA.java that contains public, protected, and private variables, along with a public method that returns the value of the private variable x3.

LISTING 5.2: ClassA.java

```
public class ClassA
{
    public int x1 = 1;
    protected int x2 = 2;
    private int x3 = 3;

    public ClassA() {}

    public void display()
    {
        System.out.println("ClassA x1: "+x1);
        System.out.println("ClassA x2: "+x2);
        System.out.println("ClassA x3: "+x3);
        System.out.println("ClassA x3: "+getX3());
        System.out.println();
    }

    public int getX3()
    {
        return(this.x3);
    }

    public static void main(String args[])
    {
        ClassA a1 = new ClassA();
        a1.display();
    }
}
```

Listing 5.2 defines the class ClassA and a main() method that initializes the variable a1 as an instance of ClassA. The next portion of the main() method invokes the display() method that prints the values of the variables x1, x2, and x3 that are public, protected, and private variables, respectively. Launch the code in Listing 5.2 and you will see the following output:

```
ClassA x1:  1
ClassA x2:  2
ClassA x3:  3
ClassA x3:  3
```

Notice that there are two ways to access the value of the variable x3: one way is to invoke this.x3 and the other way is to invoke the getX3() method.

In general, the latter method is preferred, which means that you need to write "getters" and "setters" for any variables in your Java code that need to be exposed and made available.

Another point to remember: if `classB` is a subclass of `classA`, then the keyword `this` in `classB` *cannot* access variables in `classA`, which means that you need to invoke an accessor method (you will see an example later in this chapter).

IDENTITY AND EQUALITY ARE DIFFERENT CONCEPTS

Suppose that the variables `a1` and `a2` are both instances of a class `A`. There are several possibilities regarding `a1` and `a2`:

1. `a1` and `a2` contain different values
2. `a1` and `a2` contain the same values and reside in different memory locations
3. `a1` and `a2` contain the same values and reside in the same memory location

In case #1, we know that `a1` is *not equal* to `a2`, which means that the following code snippet is true:

```
if(a1 != a2) { . . . }
```

In case #2, `a1` and `a2` are an example of *equality*, which means that the following code snippet evaluates to `true`:

```
if(a1.equals(a2) { . . . }
```

In case #3, `a1` and `a2` are an example of *identity*, which means that the following code snippet evaluates to `true`:

```
if(a1 == a2) { . . . }
```

The `Object` class (discussed in more detail later in this chapter) provides the methods `equals()` and `hashCode()` as a default mechanism for determining the identity of each instance of a class. However, you can override either of these methods if you want to change the definition of the identity of an instance of a class. Listing 5.3 displays the content of `MyEmployee.java` that illustrates the preceding concepts.

LISTING 5.3: *MyEmployee.java*

```
public class MyEmployee
{
  private String fname;
  private String lname;
  private String empId;

  public MyEmployee(String fname, String lname, String empId)
  {
```

```java
      this.fname = fname;
      this.lname = lname;
      this.empId = empId;

    System.out.println("Employee: "+fname+" "+lname+" "+empId);
  }

  // override the default equals() method:
  public boolean equals(Object o)
  {
     if (o == this) return true;

     if (o == null || this.getClass() != o.getClass())
       return false;

     MyEmployee that = (MyEmployee)o;

     return ( (this.fname.compareTo(that.fname) == 0) &&
              (this.lname.compareTo(that.lname) == 0) &&
              (this.empId.compareTo(that.empId) == 0) );
  }

  @Override
  public int hashCode()
  {
     // return a calculated value such as a memory
     // address of the Object on which it is invoked

     // all return the same value for emp1/emp2/emp3:
     // return this.fname.hashCode();
     // return (this.fname+this.lname).hashCode();
     String key = this.fname+this.lname+this.empId;
     return key.hashCode();

     // this code snippet causes a stack overflow error:
     // return this.hashCode();
  }

  public static void main(String[] args)
  {
     MyEmployee emp1 = new MyEmployee("Sally","Jones","1000");
     MyEmployee emp2 = new MyEmployee("Sally","Jones","1000");
     MyEmployee emp3 = emp1;
     MyEmployee emp4 = new MyEmployee("Sally","Smith","1000");

     System.out.println("");

     if(emp1 == emp2)
     {
        System.out.println("emp1==emp2 is true");
     }
     else
     {
        System.out.println("emp1==emp2 is false");
     }

     if(emp1.equals(emp2))
     {
```

```
            System.out.println("emp1.equals(emp2) is true");
        }
        else
        {
            System.out.println("emp1.equals(emp2) is false");
        }

        System.out.println("");

        if(emp1 == emp3)
        {
            System.out.println("emp1==emp3 is true");
        }
        else
        {
            System.out.println("emp1==emp3 is false");
        }

        if(emp1.equals(emp3))
        {
            System.out.println("emp1.equals(emp3) is true");
        }
        else
        {
            System.out.println("emp1.equals(emp3) is false");
        }
        System.out.println("");
        System.out.println("emp1 hashcode: "+emp1.hashCode());
        System.out.println("emp2 hashcode: "+emp2.hashCode());
        System.out.println("emp3 hashcode: "+emp3.hashCode());
        System.out.println("emp4 hashcode: "+emp4.hashCode());
    }
}
```

Listing 5.3 defines the class MyEmployee and a main() method that initializes the variables emp1, emp2, and emp3 as instances of the MyEmployee class. Since emp1 and emp2 contain different values, they are different instances that occupy different locations in memory. However, emp1 and emp3 have the same contents and also the same memory location because of the way that emp3 is initialized.

The equals() method is overridden, and it determines whether two instances of the MyEmployee class are the same instance. The next portion of the main() method contains multiple conditional logic statements to make various comparisons whose output is displayed later. Now launch the code in Listing 5.3 and you will see the following output:

```
Employee: Sally Jones 1000
Employee: Sally Jones 1000

emp1==emp2 is false
emp1.equals(emp2) is true

emp1==emp3 is true
emp1.equals(emp3) is true
```

```
emp1 hashcode: 1959690635
emp2 hashcode: 1959690635
emp3 hashcode: 1959690635
emp4 hashcode: -336423593
```

If you need additional confirmation that the default methods have been overridden, perform the following steps:

1. Comment out the `equals()` method.
2. Comment out the `hashCode()` method.
3. Recompile the modified code.

When you launch the recompiled code, you will see the following (different) output:

```
Employee: Sally Jones 1000
Employee: Sally Jones 1000

emp1==emp2 is false
emp1.equals(emp2) is false

emp1==emp3 is true
emp1.equals(emp3) is true

emp1 hashcode: 2055281021
emp2 hashcode: 523429237
emp3 hashcode: 2055281021
emp4 hashcode: 664740647
```

Notice the **false** that is shown in bold: this differs from the previous block of output that is generated when you override the `equals()` method versus using the default `equals()` method. In addition, the hash code values are different in the two corresponding blocks of output. The key point to remember: if you need to override the `equals()` method in your class, specify a condition that uniquely determines each instance of your class.

A QUICK INTRODUCTION TO INHERITANCE

Although the fundamental concept of inheritance in OOP is straightforward, there are some aspects of inheritance that might be confusing if you are new to this concept. Let's consider a Venn diagram with two circles A and B, and that A is a proper subset of B. Thus, B has everything that's in A, but there are things in B that are not in A. From a set theoretic perspective, A is a subset of B; however, from the standpoint of OOP, B is a *subclass* of A.

*Here is the key point: an instance of class A can be **replaced** by an instance of class B, but an instance of class B **cannot** be replaced with an instance of class A.*

With the preceding thought in mind, let's look at Listing 5.4 that displays the content of SubClassB that is a subclass of ClassA that is defined in Listing 5.2.

LISTING 5.4: SubClassB.java

```
public class SubClassB extends ClassA
{
    public SubClassB() {}

    public void display()
    {
        // public and protected vars are accessible
        System.out.println("SubClassB x1: "+x1);
        System.out.println("SubClassB x2: "+x2);

        // private var is accessible via an accessor
        System.out.println("SubClassB x3: "+this.getX3());
        System.out.println();

        //error: x3 is a private variable
        //System.out.println("SubClassB x3: "+x3);
    }

    public static void main(String args[])
    {
        ClassA a1 = new ClassA();
        a1.display();

        SubClassB b1 = new SubClassB();
        b1.display();

        ClassA b2 = new SubClassB();
        b2.display();
        ((ClassA) b2).display();

        //error:
        //((SubClassB) a1).display();
    }
}
```

Listing 5.4 defines the class `SubClassB` and a `main()` method that initializes the variable `a1` as an instance of `ClassA`. The next portion of the `main()` method invokes the `display()` method that prints the values of the variables `x1`, `x2`, and `x3` that are `public`, `protected`, and `private`, respectively. Since `x3` is a private variable in `classA`, the value of `x3` can only be obtained via an accessor method.

The next portion of the `main()` method initializes the variable `b1` as an instance of the class `SubClassB`, and then invokes the `display()` method in `SubClassB`.

Lastly, the `main()` method *declares* the variable `b2` to be of type `ClassA`, but it's *instantiated* as an instance of the class `SubClassB`, and then invokes the `display()` method in `SubClassB`. Notice how the following code snippet casts `b2` as an instance of `ClassA` and then invokes the `display()` method, as shown here:

```
((ClassA) b2).display();
```

Although you might be tempted to think that the display() method in ClassA is invoked, in actuality, the display() method in SubClassB is invoked. Launch the code in Listing 5.4 and you will see the following output:

```
ClassA x1:  1
ClassA x2:  2
ClassA x3:  3

SubClassB x1:  1
SubClassB x2:  2
SubClassB x3:  3

SubClassB x1:  1
SubClassB x2:  2
SubClassB x3:  3

SubClassB x1:  1
SubClassB x2:  2
SubClassB x3:  3
```

Notice the last snippet of commented out code in Listing 5.4: if you uncomment this code, you will get a compilation error because a1 is an instance of ClassA but not an instance of SubClassB. As we noted earlier, an instance of SubClassB cannot be replaced by an instance of ClassA; therefore, a1 cannot be cast as an instance of SubClassB.

Recall that if B is a subclass of A, then B has access to the non-private members (i.e., public or protected) of A, but A does not have access to any members of B. In the case of subclasses, constructors are invoked in a sequence that starts from the parent class and then "downward" to the subclasses.

For example, suppose that A is a class, and B is a subclass of A, and C is a subclass of B. When an instance of C is created, the sequence of constructor invocations is A, then B, and then C.

The final Modifier with Java Methods and Classes

You can prevent a method in class A from being overridden in class B by designating that method as final. In general, you can also prevent a class from being subclassed by declaring that class as final. When would this functionality be useful? Suppose that you give someone a JAR file that contains compiled Java classes but nothing is declared as final. Then the other person can import your classes and override your code by defining subclasses of your classes.

WORKING WITH VALUE OBJECTS IN JAVA

A *value object* is a Java class that only keeps track of the attributes of a logical entity, which typically involves setters and getters and a constructor. For example, suppose a student registers for multiple courses, and you want to keep track of those courses.

In simplified terms, a course contains attributes for its name, its description, and number of credits for the course. Hence, each course can be maintained via a value object because you will not perform any operations on the name, description, or the number of credits. As a result, you only need to create an instance of this class that you can add to the list of courses for each student.

Entities and value objects often have a master/detail relationship, such as PurchaseOrder and LineItem, Employee and Department, Person and Address, and also Customer and PurchaseOrder. Some entities can contain references to multiple entities and/or value objects. For example, a Customer can have multiple PurchaseOrder instances, each of which can contain one or more LineItem entities.

However, Student and Course have a many-to-many relationship because a single student can enroll in multiple courses, and a single course can have multiple students enrolled. Similar comments apply to the relationship between Users and Movies.

AN EXAMPLE OF A VALUE OBJECT IN JAVA

The previous section provided a high-level description of entities and value objects. This section contains a concrete example of a value object in the file LongEmployee.java that contains attributes of an employee, such as an employee's first name, last name, address-related information, and employee-specific details. If you created a relational database table for this class, it would be completely denormalized.

The code in this section represents the "brute force" definition that does not take into account any logical relationships among the attributes in this class. A subsequent section shows you how to normalize LongEmployee into the four classes Employee.java, EmpDetails.java, Person.java, and Address.java (in Chapter 1). These four Java classes are actually value objects that contain only logically related attributes.

Listing 5.5 displays the content of LongEmployee.java that defines eight private variables and a constructor with eight parameters that correspond to the eight private variables.

LISTING 5.5: LongEmployee.java

```java
public class LongEmployee
{
    private String firstName;
    private String lastName;

    private String street;
    private String city;
    private String state;

    private String empId;
    private int grade;
    private double years;
```

```
public LongEmployee(String firstName, String
lastName,String street, String city, String state,
String empId, int grade, double years)
{
    this.firstName = firstName;
    this.lastName  = lastName;

    this.street = street;
    this.city   = city;
    this.state  = state;

    this.empId = empId;
    this.grade = grade;
    this.years = years;
}

public void printDetails()
{
    System.out.println("First Name: "+firstName);
    System.out.println("Last Name:  "+lastName);
    System.out.println("Street:     "+street);
    System.out.println("City:       "+city);
    System.out.println("State:      "+state);
    System.out.println("ID:         "+empId);
    System.out.println("Grade:      "+grade);
    System.out.println("Years:      "+years);
    System.out.println();
}

public static void main (String args[])
{
    LongEmployee e1 = new LongEmployee(
                    "John", "Smith",
                    "1234 Main St", "Chicago", "IL",
                    "2000", 10, 5);

    LongEmployee e2 = new LongEmployee(
                    "Jane", "Andrews",
                    "1234 Oak Ave", "Newport", "CA",
                    "2000", 10, 5);

    e1.printDetails();
    e2.printDetails();
}
}
```

Listing 5.5 defines the class LongEmployee and a main() method that instantiates the objects e1 and e2, both of which are instances of LongEmployee, by invoking the constructor with the eight private variables that are defined at the top of Listing 5.5.

The second portion of the main() method invokes the printDetails() method for e1 and then for e2 to display the values that are stored in e1 and e2, as shown below:

```
First Name: John
Last Name:   Smith
```

```
Street:       1234 Main St
City:         Chicago
State:        IL
ID:           2000
Grade:        10
Years:        5.0

First Name:   Jane
Last Name:    Andrews
Street:       1234 Oak Ave
City:         Newport
State:        CA
ID:           2000
Grade:        10
Years:        5.0
```

At this point, you have a rudimentary understanding of inheritance, getters and setters, and the scope of variables in a Java class. We can now explore the concept of interfaces, which is discussed in the next section.

WHAT IS A JAVA INTERFACE?

Java supports the concept of an *interface*, which specifies the name and return type of one or more methods, along with constants (which is optional). In more recent versions of Java, you can define a sub-interface of an interface, and you can also specify a default method to execute in the interface.

An interface contains the signature of one or more methods (but empty interfaces exist, such as `Serializable`) and possibly constants. Prior to Java 8, only a class could contain the implementation of the methods in an interface (via the `implements` keyword), whereas Java 8 supports method implementations in Java 8 interfaces.

Java supports single inheritance of classes and multiple inheritance of interfaces. For example, suppose that `MyClass` extends the class `MyBase` (defined in `MyBase.java`) and also implements the interface `BaseInfo` (defined in `BaseInfo.java`). Then `MyClass.java` will contain the following code snippet:

```
public class MyClass extends MyBase implements BaseInfo
{
    // code goes here
}
```

Extending Interfaces

Java also enables you to define an interface that extends an existing interface. For example, the interface `MyArrayMethods2` extends the interface `MyArrayMethods`, as shown here:

```
public interface MyArrayMethods2 extends MyArrayMethods
{
    void basicMethod2();
}
```

This functionality is convenient when you cannot modify an existing interface to include new methods; simply extend the existing interface and then you can define classes that implement the newly created interface.

Java Interfaces and Abstract Classes

Java supports the concept of an *abstract class*, which means that that class contains at least one *abstract method*, where the latter is a method signature without any code. If class A contains an abstract method, then you cannot create an instance of class A; you must first define a subclass B of class A such that B implements the code for the abstract method(s) in A. At this point, you can create an instance of class B. The same situation is true if class A has multiple abstract methods.

In the event that class A contains *only* abstract methods, then class A is called a *pure abstract class*. Later in this chapter, you will see code samples involving Java interfaces and abstract classes.

A JAVA CLASS THAT IMPLEMENTS AN INTERFACE

Listing 5.6 displays the content of MyArrayMethods.java that is an interface that specifies the methods implemented in ArrayExamples3.java.

LISTING 5.6: MyArrayMethods.java

```
public interface MyArrayMethods
{
    void initializeArrays();
    void calculateTotals();
    void displayCelsiusResults();
    void displayNames();
    String getFirstName();
}
```

Listing 5.6 defines the interface called MyArrayMethods that contains four methods with no parameters and a return type of void. The fifth method defines a method with no parameters and a return type of String.

Listing 5.7 displays the content of ArrayExamples4.java that implements the interface that is defined in MyArrayMethods.java.

LISTING 5.7: ArrayExamples4.java

```
public class ArrayExamples4 implements MyArrayMethods
{
    private int arraySize = 12;
    private int maxCelsius = 40;
    private double intSumCelsius = 0;
    private double intAvgCelsius = 0;
    private double dblSumCelsius = 0.0;
    private double dblAvgCelsius = 0.0;

    private double[] celsiusValues = new double[arraySize];
```

```java
   private int[] celsiusValues2 = new int[arraySize];
   private String[] names = {"Tic", "Tac", "Toe"};

   public ArrayExamples4()
   {
      initializeArrays();
      calculateTotals();
      displayCelsiusResults();
      displayNames();
   }

  public void initializeArrays()
  {
     // initialize arrays with random values
     for(int i=0; i<arraySize; i++)
     {
        celsiusValues[i]  = maxCelsius*Math.random();
        celsiusValues2[i] = (int)celsiusValues[i];
     }
  }

  public void calculateTotals()
  {
     // calculate the array sums
     for(int i=0; i<arraySize; i++)
     {
        intSumCelsius += celsiusValues2[i];
        dblSumCelsius += celsiusValues[i];
     }

     dblAvgCelsius = dblSumCelsius/arraySize;
     intAvgCelsius = (int)(intSumCelsius/arraySize);
  }

  public void displayCelsiusResults()
  {
     System.out.println("Total Celsius    "+dblSumCelsius);
     System.out.println("Avg Celsius:     "+dblAvgCelsius);
     System.out.println("Total Celsius2: "+intSumCelsius);
     System.out.println("Avg Celsius2:    "+intAvgCelsius);
     System.out.println();
  }

  public void displayNames()
  {
     // display the contents of the names array:
     for(int i=0; i<names.length; i++)
     {
        System.out.println("Name "+(i+1)+": "+names[i]);
     }
  }

  public String getFirstName()
  {
     return names[0];
  }

public static void main(String args[])
```

```
    {
      ArrayExamples4 ae4 = new ArrayExamples4();

      String name0 = ae4.getFirstName();
      System.out.println("First name: "+name0);
    }
}
```

Listing 5.7 contains almost the same code that you saw in Listing 5.5: the only change is the first line (shown in bold) that declares the `ArrayExamples4` class as an implementation of the interface `MyArrayMethods`. Launch the code in Listing 5.7 and you will see the same output as `ArrayExamples2` in the previous section.

```
Name 1:          Tic
Name 2:          Tac
Name 3:          Toe
Total Celsius    249.4551395046531
Avg Celsius:     20.787928292054424
Total Celsius2:  243.0
Avg Celsius2:    20.0
```

JAVA ABSTRACT METHODS AND CLASSES

An *abstract method* is a method that does not contain code. A `Java` class can contain:

1. All concrete methods
2. A mixtures of concrete and abstract methods
3. All abstract methods

Only classes of type #1 in the preceding list can be instantiated directly: the other two types must *first* be subclassed by a class `B` that implements all the abstract methods, and then the implementation class `B` can be instantiated directly. You can create an instance of class `B` in exactly the same manner that you create an instance of any other `Java` class.

The following code block is an example of an abstract class that would be defined in the file `A.java`:

```
public class A {
    int   anInstanceVariable;

    public abstract int methodMustBeImplemented();

    public void doSomething() {
       // insert some code here
    }
}
```

The following code block is an example of a concrete class B that would be defined in the file `B.java`:

```
public class B extends A {
   public int methodMustBeImplemented() {
     // we *must* implement this method
   }
}
```

The following code snippet causes a compilation error because you *cannot* initialize a variable as an instance of an abstract class:

```
Object asc = new A(); // error
```

However, the following code snippet *is* valid because the variable `Binst` is an instance of a concrete class:

```
Object Binst = new B(); // valid
```

As you saw earlier in this chapter, an *abstract class* is a class that contains only abstract methods, which is discussed in the next subsection.

An Abstract Class in Java

As mentioned in the previous section, an `abstract` class A is a class that contains only abstract methods, and the keyword `abstract` is specified in the declaration of the class A. An example of an abstract class is shown here:

```
public abstract class AnAbstractClass { . . .}
```

The preceding class definition indicates that `AnAbstractClass` contains only abstract methods, and therefore a subclass must implement all of those abstract methods.

```
abstract class MyFirstAbstractClass

{
   public abstract int methodOne();
   public abstract int methodTwo();
   public abstract String methodThree();
}

public class MyConcreteSubClass extends
MyFirstAbstractClass
{
   public int methodOne() {
     // we *must* implement this method
     return 0;
   }

   public int methodTwo () {
     // we *must* implement this method
```

```
        return 0;
    }

    public String methodThree() {
        // we *must* implement this method
        return "0";
    }
}
```

Are Subclasses Always Concrete Classes in Java?

In a word, the answer to this question is "no." For example, suppose that we have the following sequence of subclasses in `Java`:

- Class `Base` contains one or more abstract methods
- Class `Sub1` is a subclass of `Base`
- Class `Sub2` is a subclass of `Sub1`
- . . .
- Class `SubN` is a subclass of `SubN-1`
- Class `Concrete1` is a subclass of `SubN`

Moreover, suppose that classes `Sub1` through `SubN` contain abstract methods. Based on earlier comments, we cannot create an instance `Base` or `Sub1` through `SubN`. However, we *can* instantiate class `Concrete1` because it's a concrete class. Eventually, this chain of subclasses must terminate with a concrete class. Otherwise, we will never be able to instantiate the last class in the chain, in which case, what would be the point of constructing such a sequence of subclasses?

Method Arguments and Interfaces

In general, specify interfaces instead of concrete implementations as arguments to a method. This allows you to invoke the same method with different concrete classes. In addition, you can make changes to the code in the method without changing the signature of the method. Thus, you can provide people with your new and updated code without modifying the signature of your methods.

Any method that has an interface as a parameter would then cast that interface to the appropriate type of concrete class to access the methods inside the concrete class.

However, we can also make a reasonable case for using an abstract class instead of an interface. Both approaches involve tradeoffs, so it's a question of which tradeoffs are most beneficial for your code base. A very good article that discusses the tradeoffs is available online:

http://hannesdorfmann.com/android/library-abstract-class

WHAT IS OOP?

The material prior to this section described interfaces and abstract classes with a `Java`-specific perspective, which provided you with a good foundation for OOP. In this section, you will learn about OOP concepts from a general viewpoint, which means that they are applicable to other programming languages.

As a starting point, a *class* is a group of functions and data, called methods and properties, respectively, that can have different types of accessibility via the utilization of specific Java keywords. An *instance* of a class is a concrete object that has state and identity.

With the preceding in mind, there are several important OOP concepts that you need to know:

- Inheritance
- Delegation
- Encapsulation
- Polymorphism

The term *inheritance* refers to the relationship between two classes A and B: if class B is a subclass of A, then we say that class B inherits from A.

The term *delegation* refers to composition of objects. For instance, if class A contains instances of classes B, C, and D, then class A can delegate different blocks of functionality to each of those classes.

The term *encapsulation* refers to performing a set of operations inside a method of a class in such a way that the code is not visible to other methods and classes.

The term *polymorphism* involves a class that can "act" as different classes. For example, if class A has subclass B and class B has subclass C, then an instance of class C can function as an instance of class B and also as an instance of class A.

In addition, there are many patterns that exist in software, and you can find entire books devoted to a description of software patterns for different languages.

INHERITANCE

If class B is a subclass of A, then B contains all the methods and properties of class A. If a method in class A has the desired behavior, then we do not need to define that same method in class B. Just to make things simpler, let's assume that both classes are concrete classes. If the method `perimeter()` exists in class A, then the same method is accessible in class B.

If we have a concrete instance of class B called `Binst` and we invoke the code snippet `Binst.perimeter()`, then Java will look for `perimeter()` in class B; since it's not defined in class B, then Java will search upward through the inheritance "chain" until it finds `perimeter()`, which is defined in class A.

Moreover, suppose that `Ainst` is an instance of class A. Since class B is a subclass of A, any instance of A can be replaced with an instance of class B. Consequently, the code snippet `Ainst.perimeter()` can be replaced with `Binst.perimeter()`.

Here is a simple example from geometry, where a rectangle is a polygon with four sides, and a square is a polygon with four sides of equal length and four equal interior angles of 90 degrees.

A square is a special case of a rectangle (or the latter is a generalization of the former). Hence, rectangles consist of squares and other four-sided polygons that are not squares. Therefore, the set of squares is a *subset* of the set of rectangles, but squares are a *subclass* of rectangles.

In the two classes defined below, both have a constructor (no code is provided yet), and both have a `perimeter()` method.

```
public class Rectangle
{
    public int width, length;
    public Rectangle() { ... }
    public double perimeter() { . . . }
}

public class Square
{
    public int side;
    public Square() { ... }
    public double perimeter() { . . . }
}
```

The following code snippet contains the `extends` keyword to indicate that `Square` is a subclass of the `Rectangle` class:

```
public class Square extends Rectangle { . . . }
```

The Java Object Class

The top-level class in the `Java` class hierarchy is the class `Object`, and all other `Java` classes inherit from the `Object` class. The `Object` class defines behavior specific to all objects in the `Java` class hierarchy. As you progress down the chain of classes (starting from the `Object` class), additional information is specified and so each class will serve a more specific purpose. Conversely, lower-level classes have more concrete functionality, whereas higher-level classes tend to have more abstract concepts.

Inheritance and Overriding Methods

In OOP, you can define a method that has the same signature (name and number and type of arguments) as a method defined in a subclass or a superclass. This situation is called *overriding* a class method.

For example, the classes `Square` and `Rectangle` both contain the `perimeter()` method, this means that the definition of `perimeter()` in `Square` overrides the definition of `perimeter()` in `Rectangle`.

If the class `Square` did not contain the definition of `perimeter()` and this method is invoked from an instance of the class `Square`, then `Java` handles this situation as follows: starting from the bottom of the class hierarchy and moving upward, the first occurrence of the method definition is the method that is executed. As you will see later in this chapter, it's also possible to explicitly invoke the overridden method in a superclass.

ENCAPSULATION

Encapsulation involves the use of accessors and mutators in order to "shield" the internal properties (such as variables) of a Java class from other classes. The use of accessors also enables you to refactor code in a Java class without modifying public APIs. Hence, other classes can access the values of properties (through accessors) without knowing how those properties were calculated.

Encapsulation refers to separating or isolating the internal details of a class from the "outside world." Encapsulation is important because it prevents other programmers from modifying the internal details of a class, which in turn can change the intended behavior of the methods in a class, and perhaps even cause them to fail.

By way of analogy, the engine in your car is "encapsulated" so that you don't need to know (or understand) the internal details. In theory, your engine can be replaced by another engine without requiring you to understand the internal workings of the new engine.

Another example is your cell phone: whenever you upgrade the hardware or download later versions of the internal software, you generally do not know the specific detail of the new functionality (or the bugs that have been fixed). Hence, encapsulation enables you to make internal changes without affecting the rest of the system (such as other classes).

As a simple illustration, the Person.java class (defined in Chapter 1) defines a person with two attributes: a first name and a last name, both of which are private String variables. This class defines two public accessor methods by which other classes can retrieve the first name and the last name of an instance of the Person class.

POLYMORPHISM

Polymorphism means "having many forms." For example, a person can have multiple roles: a student of one class and also a teacher of a different class. Through polymorphism, we can perform an action in multiple ways in different classes, all of which implement the same interface. For example, the interface Mammal can be implemented by a Cat class, a Dog class, and a Lion class. If the Mammal interface contains the method speak(), then the three preceding classes each have their own implementation of this method, which might emit the text "Meow," "Woof," and "Roar."

As you know from Listing 5.4, we can replace a class by a subclass in an assignment statement when those classes have an inheritance relationship, which is reproduced here:

```
ClassA b2 = new SubClassB();
b2.display();
((ClassA) b2).display();
```

In the preceding code block, the left-side of the assignment statement is a parent (super) class of the right-side of an assignment, so you can do the following:

- the left-side class can be replaced by a super class of the right-side class or the right-side class itself
- the left-side instance only "sees" methods in the left-side class
- the left-side instance must be cast as a right-side class to "see" methods in the right-side class

Listing 5.8, Listing 5.9, and Listing 5.10 display the contents of `BaseClass2.java`, `SubClassA.java`, and `SubclassB.java`, respectively. Note that the class `BaseClass2.java` has a subclass called `SubClassC.java`, which in turn has a subclass called `SubclassD.java`.

LISTING 5.8: BaseClass2.java

```
public class BaseClass2
{
    public BaseClass2()
    {
        System.out.println("Inside BaseClass2");
    }

    public void greetings()
    {
        System.out.println("Greetings from BaseClass2");
    }

    public void hello()
    {
        System.out.println("Hello from BaseClass2");
    }

    public static void main(String[] args)
    {
        BaseClass2 bc = new BaseClass2();
    }
}
```

Listing 5.8 defines the class `BaseClass2`, a non-empty constructor, two simple methods, and a `main()` method that initializes the variable `bc` as an instance of `BaseClass2`. The constructor of `BaseClass2` is then invoked, which displays the string `Inside BaseClass2`. Notice that neither of the methods `greetings()` or `hello()` is invoked.

LISTING 5.9: SubClassC.java

```
public class SubClassC extends BaseClass2
{
    public SubClassC()
```

```
    {
       System.out.println("Inside SubClassC");
    }

    public void hello()
    {
       System.out.println("Hello from SubClassC");
    }

    public void goodbye()
    {
       System.out.println("Goodbye from SubClassC");
    }

    public static void main(String[] args)
    {
       System.out.println("Invocation #1");
       SubClassC c1 = new SubClassC();
       c1.hello();
       System.out.println();

       System.out.println("Invocation #2");
       BaseClass2 b1 = new SubClassC();
       b1.hello();
       System.out.println();

       System.out.println("Invocation #3");
       ((SubClassC)b1).goodbye();
       System.out.println();

       // this causes an error:
       //((SubClassD)b1).goodbye();

       System.out.println("Invocation #4");
       BaseClass2 b2 = new SubClassD();
       b2.hello();
       System.out.println();

       System.out.println("Invocation #5");
       ((SubClassD)b2).goodbye();
       System.out.println();

       // this causes an error:
       //b2.goodbye();
    }
}
```

Listing 5.9 defines the class SubClassC, a non-empty constructor, and two simple methods, along with a main() method that initializes the variable c1 as an instance of SubClassC. When the constructor is invoked, the string Inside SubClassC is displayed. Next, the code snippet c1.hello() invokes the hello() method of SubClassC, which displays the string Hello from SubClassC.

Now we're going to discuss the more interesting portion of the code. The following code snippet declares b1 of type BaseClass2, but then initializes b1 as an instance of SubClassC and then invokes the hello() method:

```
BaseClass2 b1 = new SubClassC();
b1.hello();
```

What is the output of the preceding code snippet? Will it invoke the `hello()` method of `BaseClass2` or the `hello()` method of `SubClassC`?

The following code snippet casts `b1` as an instance of `SubClassC` and then invokes the `hello()` method:

```
((SubClassC)b1).goodbye();
```

The preceding snippet invokes the `hello()` method of `SubClassC`, which is a reasonable inference. However, the following snippet will not work, despite its similarity to the preceding code snippet (`SubClassD` is defined in Listing 5.10):

```
//((SubClassD)b1).goodbye();
```

The preceding code snippet *fails* for the following reason: even though `SubClassD` extends `SubClassC`, it's not substitutable for `SubClassC` because `SubClassD` can contain methods that are not visible to `SubClassC`.

The next code snippet declares `b2` of type `BaseClass2` and then initializes `b2` as an instance of `BaseClassD`, which is valid because `BaseClassD` is defined as a subclass of `BaseClass2`:

```
BaseClass2 b2 = new SubClassD();
b2.hello();
((SubClassD)b2).goodbye();
```

Before we can launch the code in Listing 5.9, we need to define the class `SubClassD`, which is displayed in Listing 5.10.

LISTING 5.10: SubClassD.java

```
public class SubClassD extends SubClassC
{
    public SubClassD()
    {
        System.out.println("Inside SubClassD");
    }

    public void hello()
    {
        System.out.println("Hello from SubClassD");
    }

    public void goodbye()
    {
        System.out.println("Goodbye from SubClassD");
    }

    public static void main(String[] args)
    {
        SubClassD sd = new SubClassD();
        sd.greetings();
    }
}
```

Listing 5.10 defines the class `SubClassD` and a `main()` method that initializes the variable `sd` as an instance of `SubClassD`. The constructor is then invoked, which displays the string `Goodbye from SubClassD`.

Next, the snippet `sd.greetings()` invokes the `greetings()` method, which is not defined in `SubClassD` (defined in Listing 5.9), nor is it defined in `SubClassC`, which is the parent class of `SubClassD`.

In fact, the `greetings()` method is defined in `BaseClass2`, which is the parent class of `SubClassC`. The `greetings()` method displays the following string:

```
Greetings from BaseClass2
```

Compile the classes `BaseClass2.java`, `SubClassC.java`, and `SubClassD.java`, and now run the following command:

```
java BaseClass2
```

The output from the preceding code snippet is here:

```
Inside BaseClass2
```

Next, run the following command:

```
java SubClassD
```

The output from the preceding code snippet is here:

```
Inside BaseClass2
Inside SubClassD
Greetings from BaseClass2
```

The class `SubClassD` is a subclass of `BaseClass2` that contains the method `greetings()`, whereas `SubClassD` does not contain a `greetings()` method. However, due to the inheritance relationship between `BaseClass2` and `SubClassD`, an instance of `SubClassD` can invoke the `greetings()` method, and Java will find that method in the class `BaseClass2` and then execute that method. Run the following command:

```
java SubClassC
```

The output from the preceding code snippet is here:

```
Invocation #1
Inside BaseClass2
Inside SubClassC
Hello from SubClassC

Invocation #2
Inside BaseClass2
Inside SubClassC
Hello from SubClassC
```

```
Invocation #3
Goodbye from SubClassC

Invocation #4
Inside BaseClass2
Inside SubClassD
Hello from SubClassD

Invocation #5
Goodbye from SubClassD
```

The interesting code is in the `main()` routine of `SubClassC`. The next section explains which code is correct and which code is incorrect, followed by a set of rules that enable you to determine the correctness of an assignment statement.

The following code snippet is correct because `c1` is an instance of `SubClassC`:

```
SubClassC c1 = new SubClassC();
```

You can replace the class on the left-side of the preceding code snippet with a super class. Since `BaseClass2` is a super class of `SubClassC`, the code in #2 is correct:

```
BaseClass2 b1 = new SubClassC();
```

Next, `b1` was instantiated with the class `SubClassC` on the right-hand side, which means that we can "downcast" `b1` as an instance of `SubClassC`, so the code in #3 is correct:

```
((SubClassC)b1).goodbye();
```

However, `SubClassD` is *not* a super class of `SubClassC`, and obviously it does not equal `SubClassC`, so this line of code is incorrect:

```
//((SubClassD)b1).goodbye();
```

Since `BaseClass2` is a super class of `SubClassD`, the code in #4 is correct:

```
BaseClass2 b2 = new SubClassD();
```

Next, `b2` was instantiated with the class `SubClassD` on the right-hand side, which means that we can "downcast" `b2` as an instance of `SubClassD` (so that it can be used like an instance of `SubClassD`), and consequently the code in #5 is correct:

```
((SubClassD)b2).goodbye();
```

The final code snippet is *incorrect* because `BaseClass2` does *not* contain a `goodbye()` method, and the instance variable `b2` "behaves" like an instance of `BaseClass2`:

```
//b2.goodbye();
```

SUMMARY

This chapter introduced you to additional `Java` features, such as overloading methods and the difference between identity and equality. Next, you learned about inheritance, along with the `final` modifier for methods and variables.

In addition, you learned about interfaces, and the fact that a `Java` class can implement multiple interfaces but can only have a single parent class. You also learned about abstract classes and how they differ from interfaces.

Moreover, you were introduced to encapsulation and polymorphism, which are two other fundamental concepts in OOP.

CHAPTER 6

DATA STRUCTURES

This chapter introduces various built-in data structures in Java, such as hash maps and linked lists, and also how to use some of the Java classes that belong to the Java Collections classes.

The first part of this chapter discusses some of the legacy Java classes that have been superseded by classes in the Collection framework, followed by an overview of Iterators.

The second part of this chapter delves into some of the most common Collection classes, along with code samples that use those classes to find the distinct characters in a text string. The benefit of solving the same task using different collection-related cases enables you to compare the code that is required for solving the same task.

The final part of this chapter discusses some of the useful methods in the Java 8 enhancement for the Collection classes. The code samples are intended to provide a basic understanding of how to use Collection-related classes, and therefore they have not been optimized for performance.

Let's briefly explore some legacy Java classes for data structures, along with some newer classes that supplant the legacy classes.

JAVA LEGACY DATA STRUCTURES

The Java utility package provides the following interface and classes that are legacy classes: BitSet, Dictionary, Enumeration, Hashtable, Properties, Stack, and Vector. Starting with version 2, Java introduced a framework called the Collection Framework.

Note: The legacy data structures Vector and Hashtable are synchronized, whereas the classes in the Collection framework in Java 7 are not synchronized.

Unsynchronized Java classes are not thread-safe and are intended for situations that do not involve race conditions from multiple threads. For example, read-only operations do not require synchronization. As a result, such classes tend to be simpler and also have better performance.

One benefit of the Collection framework is its support for thread-safe counterparts to the unsynchronized classes in case you need such functionality. Before delving into Collections, let's take a brief tour of Iterators, with code samples that illustrate different iteration techniques that have been used during different releases of Java.

ITERATORS

This section discusses the notion of an Iterator and also different types of iterators. You will see several code blocks that perform iterations in Java, starting with the earliest release of Java. If you have already worked with Iterators, then you can quickly skim this section.

What is an Iterator?

An *iterator* enables you to sequentially access all elements of a collection. In effect, an iterator allows you to iterate ("loop") over a collection of objects. You can use iterators to loop through the elements in an array, files in a directory, and the vertices of a graph. An iterator does not change a given collection, but the operations that are performed on the elements of the collection can change the collection.

Active versus Passive

In the case of an active iterator, the *client* controls the creation of an iterator as well as the iteration of an active iterator. By contrast, a passive iterator controls its iteration over a Collection. Note that active iterators were used prior to Java 8, whereas passive iterators were used in later versions of Java.

Enumeration: Oldest Style Iteration

In the initial releases of Java, the Iterator design pattern was implemented via the Enumeration class (which is part of legacy code), as shown in this example:

```
Vector words = new Vector();


// populate 'words' with some strings
// . . .

Enumeration e = words.elements();
while (e.hasMoreElements())
{
    String word = (String) e.nextElement();
    System.out.println(word);
}
```

Notice that the preceding `while` loop invokes `e.nextElement()` to access the next element in the variable `e` (which is an `Enumeration`).

Iterator: Second Style Iteration

In `Java` 1.2 through 1.4, the following code block illustrates how to use an `Iterator` to perform iteration:

```
List words = new LinkedList();


// populate 'words'
// . . .

Iterator item = words.iterator();
while (iter.hasNext()){
   String word = (String) iter.next();
   System.out.println(word);
}
```

Let's see how to use *generics* to perform iteration, as discussed in the next section.

Generics: Third Style Iteration

In `Java` 1.2 through 1.4, the following code block illustrates how to use a `for` loop to perform iteration:

```
List<String> words = new LinkedList<String>();
// populate 'words'
// . . .

for(String word: words)
{
   System.out.println(word);
}
```

`Java` 7 introduced the "diamond operator," which is shown here:

```
List<String> words = new LinkedList<>();
```

The preceding code snippet defines the variable `words` as an instance of `LinkedList` in which each element is a `String`.

Incidentally, `List` is an *interface*, whereas `LinkedList` is a concrete *class* that implements the `List` interface. Recall the explanation in Chapter 6 about substituting a subclass for a class: the same holds true when you replace an *interface* with a class that *implements* that interface.

forEach: Fourth Style Iteration

`Java` 8 supports the `forEach()` loop to perform iterations, as shown here:

```
List<String> words = new LinkedList<>();
```

```
// populate 'words'
// . . .

words.forEach(name -> System.out.println(word));
```

The preceding code block contains a *lambda expression*, which is essentially a nameless function. Lambda expressions can be useful when you need to execute a block of code that is executed only once, such as an event handler for click events on a button.

Streams: Fifth Style Iteration

Java 8 and beyond support the Stream class that involves the lazy operators and terminal operators. A *lazy operator* is an operator that is not executed immediately, whereas the execution of a *terminal operator* initiates the execution of lazy operators. A terminal operator is the final operator in a sequence of lazy operators. Here is a humorous analogy (borrowed from Venkat Subramanian) that might help in understanding the difference between lazy operators and terminal operators:

```
[Mother and two teenage sons watching television in the
living room]
Mother: "You need to take out the garbage."
Sons: [No response]
Mother [A few minutes later]: "You need to finish your
homework."
Sons: [Silence]
Mother [A few minutes later]: "I'm going to get your
father."
Sons: Leaping into immediate action. . .
```

As a short preview, the following code block involves the diamond operator to initialize the variable words, followed by an invocation of the stream() method. Method chaining invokes the filter() operator (which is a lazy operator) and then the forEach() operator (which is a terminal operator):

```
List<String> words = new LinkedList<>();
// populate 'words'
// . . .

words.stream()
     .filter(word -> word.startsWith("A"))
     .forEach(w -> System.out.println(w));
```

Now that you have a basic understanding of Iterators and Streams, let's look at the Collection interfaces, the Collection classes, and some code samples.

THE COLLECTION INTERFACES

This section contains a list of the interfaces that are defined in the Collection framework, along with a one-sentence description of their purpose. You will see code samples that involve of some of these interfaces later in the chapter.

The `Collection` interface enables you to work with groups of objects; it is at the top of the Collection hierarchy.

The `List` interface extends `Collection` and an instance of `List` stores an ordered collection of elements.

The `Set` interface contains the same methods as `Collection`, along with the constraint that a set must contain unique elements. `SortedSet` extends `Set` to handle sorted sets.

`Map` maps unique keys to values, and `Map.Entry` is an inner class of the class `Map` that describes an element (a key/value pair) in a map.

`SortedMap` extends `Map` so that the keys are maintained in ascending order.

`Enumeration` is a legacy interface and defines the methods by which you can enumerate (obtain one at a time) the elements in a collection of objects. As you saw in a previous section, the `Iterator` supersedes the `Enumeration` interface.

THE COLLECTION CLASSES

Java provides two types of collection classes that implement the `Collection` interfaces: some provide full implementations and others are abstract classes. Recall that you cannot instantiate an abstract class. First, you must extend an abstract class with a class that implements the abstract methods in the abstract class.

The `Collection` framework provides several general-purpose implementations of the core interfaces. In particular, the most common implementation for the `List`, `Map`, `Deque`, `Queue`, and `Set` interfaces are the `ArrayList`, `HashMap`, `ArrayDeque`, `LinkedList`, and `HashSet` classes, respectively.

An extensive list of the standard collection classes is here, along with a one-sentence description of their purpose:

- `AbstractCollection`: implements most of the `Collection` interface
- `AbstractList`: extends `AbstractCollection` and implements most of the `List` interface.
- `AbstractSequentialList`: extends `AbstractList` for use by a collection that uses sequential rather than random access of its elements
- `LinkedList`: implements a linked list by extending `AbstractSequentialList`
- `ArrayList`: implements a dynamic array by extending `AbstractList`
- `AbstractSet`: extends `AbstractCollection` and implements most of the `Set` interface
- `HashSet`: extends `AbstractSet` for use with a hash table
- `LinkedHashSet`: extends `HashSet` to allow insertion-order iterations
- `TreeSet`: implements a set stored in a tree. Extends `AbstractSet`
- `AbstractMap`: implements most of the `Map` interface

- `HashMap`: extends `AbstractMap` to use a hash table
- `TreeMap`: extends `AbstractMap` to use a tree
- `WeakHashMap`: extends `AbstractMap` to use a hash table with weak keys
- `LinkedHashMap`: extends `HashMap` to allow insertion-order iterations
- `IdentityHashMap`: extends `AbstractMap` and uses reference equality when comparing documents.

Later in this chapter, you will see code samples that involve some of classes in the preceding list and you can perform an online search for more information for the remaining classes.

OVERVIEW OF JAVA COLLECTIONS

As you saw earlier in this chapter, various `Java` legacy classes are synchronized, whereas the implementations in the `Collection` Framework are unsynchronized. However, the `Collection` Framework provides "wrapper" classes that are thread-safe.

The six core collection interfaces (`Collection`, `Set`, `List`, `Map`, `SortedSet`, and `SortedMap`) provide a corresponding static factory method, as shown here:

- `public static <T> Collection<T> synchronizedCollection( Collection<T> c);`
- `public static <T> Set<T> synchronizedSet(Set<T> s);`
- `public static <T> List<T> synchronizedList(List<T> list);`
- `public static <K,V> Map<K,V> synchronizedMap(Map<K,V> m);`
- `public static <T> SortedSet<T> synchronizedSortedSet(SortedSet<T> s);`
- `public static <K,V> SortedMap<K,V> synchronizedSortedMap(SortedMap<K,V> m);`

The methods in the preceding list return a *synchronized* (i.e., thread-safe) `Collection` that involves the specified "backing" collection. Note that access to the backing collection must be performed through the returned collection to ensure serial access. Create the *synchronized* collection via the following code snippet:

```
List<Type> list = Collections.synchronizedList(new
ArrayList<Type>());
```

Iterating over Wrapper-Synchronized Collections

You must manually synchronize whenever you iterate over a returned collection. This requirement arises because iteration involves multiple invocations into a collection that must be handled as a single atomic operation. Here is an example of iterating over a wrapper-synchronized collection:

```
Collection<Type> coll =
        Collections.synchronizedCollection(myCollection);
synchronized(coll) {
    for (Type elem : coll)
        someMethod(elem);
}
```

Two comments about the preceding code block. First, notice the keyword synchronized in the preceding code block: this will ensure that the code is executed in a thread-safe manner. Second, if you specify an explicit iterator, then the iterator method *must* be called invoked the synchronized block to ensure correct behavior.

CONVENIENCE IMPLEMENTATIONS

This section describes several mini-implementations that can be more convenient and efficient than general-purpose implementations when you don't need their full power. All the implementations in this section are made available via static factory methods rather than public classes.

List View of an Array

Before we look at the code, recall the following details about List and ArrayList:

- List is a Java interface.
- ArrayList is a concrete Java class.
- ArrayList implements the List interface.

As a reminder, if A is a concrete class and B is a concrete subclass of A, then instances of A can be replaced by instances of B: *this is also true when A is just an interface and B is a concrete class*. Therefore, the following code snippet is legal (and Integer can be replaced by other classes):

```
List<Integer> itemList = new ArrayList<Integer>();
```

The Arrays.asList() method returns a List view of an array so that you can pass a List of elements to other methods that requires a List parameter. Moreover, you can convert a List variable to an array via the ArrayList class, as shown here:

```
List<Integer> itemList = new ArrayList<Integer>();
itemList.add(1);
itemList.add(2);
itemList.add(3);

Integer[] array = new Integer[itemList.size()];
array = itemList.toArray(array);
```

Immutable Multiple-Copy List

Java provides the `Collections.nCopies()` method that enables you to create a `List` consisting of duplicate copies of the same element. Here is a sample invocation:

```
List<Type> myList = new ArrayList<Type>(
                    Collections.nCopies(1000, (Type)null);
```

Make sure that you replace the word `Type` in the preceding snippet with a concrete class, such as `Integer` or `Decimal`.

As a variation of the preceding code snippet, you can use the following code snippet to initialize an `ArrayList` of 1,000 null elements:

```
List<Type> list = new ArrayList<Type>(
                  Collections.nCopies(1000, (Type)null);
```

As a third example, you can append multiple copies of another string to a variable of type `List<String>`, as shown in the following code snippet:

```
myTools.addAll(Collections.nCopies(10, "hammer"));
```

In addition, the `Collections.singleton()` method returns an immutable singleton `Set` that consists of a single specified element.

THE ARRAYLIST CLASS

In the previous section, you saw an example of the `ArrayList` class. Interestingly, the `ArrayList` class has properties of an array as well as properties of a list.

Hence, the `ArrayList` supports the methods `insert()`, `remove()`, and `findAt()` that insert, remove, and find an element, respectively. These methods make `ArrayList` suitable for fast insert and delete operations.

Listing 6.1 displays the content of `ArrayListChars.java` that illustrates how to append the characters in a text string to an `ArrayList` and then display its contents. This code only appends a character that has not already been appended to the array list.

LISTING 6.1: ArrayListChars.java

```
import java.util.ArrayList;
import java.util.List;

public class ArrayListChars
{
    private char chr;
    private int charCount=0;
    private String line = "Line one and line two and three";
    private List al = new ArrayList();

    public ArrayListChars()
```

```
{
    // process each character in the current line
    for(int i=0; i<line.length(); i++)
    {
        chr = line.charAt(i);

        // check if character already exists
        boolean found = false;
        for(int j=0; j<al.size(); j++)
        {
            if((Character)al.get(j) == chr) {
                found = true;
                break;
            }
        }

        if(found == false) {
            al.add(chr);
        }
    }

    for(int i=0; i<al.size(); i++)
    {
        System.out.println("Character: "+al.get(i));
    }
}

public static void main (String args[])
{
    ArrayListChars alc1 = new ArrayListChars();
}
}
```

Listing 6.1 defines the class `ArrayListChars` whose constructor contains two `for` loops. The first `for` loop processes each character from the string variable `line`. This outer loop contains another loop to check if the current character is already stored in the variable `al`, which is an instance of the `ArrayList` class. If the current character already appears, then it is ignored; otherwise, it is appended to the variable `al`.

The second loop in the `main()` method iterates through the elements of `al` and prints their values. Launch the code in Listing 6.1 and you will see the following output:

```
Character: L
Character: i
Character: n
Character: e
Character:
Character: o
Character: a
Character: d
Character: l
Character: t
Character: w
Character: h
Character: r
```

The class `ArrayList` actually stores elements in an array; consequently, removing elements from `ArrayList` is an operation whose order is `O(n^2)`.

The next section shows you how to use a `HashMap`, which is a modern replacement for a `Hashtable`.

THE HASHMAP CLASS

The `HashMap` class uses a hash table to implement the `Map` interface. This allows the execution time of basic operations, such as `get()` and `put()`. A `HashMap` consists of key/value pairs. A search operation is very fast: given a key, you can determine its value (if it exists) in constant time. This feature obviously makes a `HashMap` well-suited for cases where fast lookup time is the most important priority.

Listing 6.2 displays the content of `HashMap1.java` that illustrates how easy it is to create a `HashMap`, add key/value pairs that have string/integer values, and then display the contents of the `HashMap`.

LISTING 6.2: HashMap1.java

```java
import java.util.HashMap;
public class HashMap1
{
    public static void main(String[] args)
    {
        var map1 = new HashMap<String, Integer>();

        map1.put("ten", 10);
        map1.put("mil", 1000000);

        var ten = map1.get("ten");
        System.out.println("ten: " + ten);
        var mil = map1.get("mil");
        System.out.println("mil: " + mil);
        System.out.println();

        for (var key : map1.keySet())
        {
            var val = map1.get(key);
            System.out.println("key/val: " + key+"/"+val);
        }
    }
}
```

Listing 6.2 defines the class `HashMap1` and a `main()` method that initializes `map1` as an instance of the `HashMap` class. Next, two key/value pairs are added to `map1`, followed by two `System.out.println()` statements that display the key/value pairs in `map1`.

The final portion of Listing 6.2 contains a `for` loop that also iterates through the elements of `map1`, which is clearly simpler than multiple `System.out.println()` statements when `map1` contains a large number of elements. Launch the code in Listing 6.2 and you will see the following output:

```
ten: 10
mil: 1000000

key/val: mil/1000000
key/val: ten/10
```

Listing 6.3 displays the content of `HashMap2.java` that illustrates how to create a `HashMap` in which the key is a string and the value associated with a given key is a list of string values.

LISTING 6.3: HashMap2.java

```java
import java.util.ArrayList;
import java.util.HashMap;
import java.util.List;
import java.util.Map;

public class HashMap2
{
    public static void main(String[] args)
    {
        // create map to store
        Map<String, List<String>> map =
                    new HashMap<String, List<String>>();

        // create list one and store values
        List<String> valSetOne = new ArrayList<String>();
        valSetOne.add("Apple");
        valSetOne.add("Antipasto");

        // create list two and store values
        List<String> valSetTwo = new ArrayList<String>();
        valSetTwo.add("Banana");

        // create list three and store values
        List<String> valSetThree = new ArrayList<String>();
        valSetThree.add("Calamari");
        valSetThree.add("Camaro");

        // put values into map
        map.put("A", valSetOne);
        map.put("B", valSetTwo);
        map.put("C", valSetThree);

        // iterate and display values
        System.out.println("Fetching Keys and [Multiple]
        Values n");
        for (Map.Entry<String, List<String>> entry : map.
        entrySet())
        {
            String key = entry.getKey();
            List<String> values = entry.getValue();
            System.out.println("Key = " + key);
            System.out.println("Values = " + values + "n");
        }
    }
}
```

Listing 6.3 defines the class `HashMap1`, whose `main()` method initializes various collection-related classes with strings and characters. The output from Listing 6.3 is here:

```
Key = A
Values = [Apple, Aeroplane]n
Key = B
Values = [Bat]n
Key = C
Values = [Cat, Car]n
```

THE HASHSET CLASS

The `HashSet` class implements the `Set` interface and is "backed" by a hash table, but does not guarantee the order in which the elements are iterated. This allows the execution time of basic operations, such as `get()` and `put()`.

A `HashSet` consists of key/value pairs. Given a specific key, it's possible to find its value (if it exists) in constant time. Hence, `HashSet` is well-suited for cases where fast lookup time is the most important priority, just as you saw with the `HashMap` class.

Listing 6.4 displays the content of `HashSetChars.java` that illustrates how to create a `HashSet` and update its contents.

LISTING 6.4: HashSetChars.java

```java
import java.util.HashSet;
import java.util.Iterator;

public class HashSetChars
{
    private char chr;
    private int charCount=0;
    private String line = "Line one and line two and three";
    private HashSet<Character> s1 = new
    HashSet<Character>();

    public HashSetChars()
    {
        // process each character in the current line
        for(int i=0; i<line.length(); i++)
        {
            chr = line.charAt(i);

            // check if character already exists
            boolean found = false;

            Iterator iter = s1.iterator();
            while (iter.hasNext())
            {
                char chr1 = (Character)iter.next();

                if(chr1 == chr) {
```

```
                        found = true;
                        break;
                }
            }

            if(found == false) {
                s1.add(chr);
            }
        }

        System.out.println("Characters: "+s1);
    }

    public static void main (String args[])
    {
        HashSetChars hsc = new HashSetChars();
    }
}
```

Listing 6.4 defines the class `HashSetChars` whose constructor contains a `for` loop that invokes the `charAt()` method to initialize the variable `chr` with a character from the `String` variable `line`.

Next, a `while` loop searches for `chr` in the `HashSet` `s1`; if it is not found, then `chr` is added to `s1`. This process is repeated for each character of the variable `line`. The output from Listing 6.4 is here:

```
Characters: [ , d, e, a, L, n, o, l, h, i, w, t, r]
```

THE LINKEDLIST CLASS

Earlier you learned that the `ArrayList` class has properties of an array as well as properties of a list: the same is true for the `LinkedList` class. Common operations for an `LinkedList` are `insert()`, `remove()`, and `get()` that insert, remove, and find an element, respectively. A `LinkedList` is useful for fast insert and delete operations.

Listing 6.5 displays the content of `LinkedListChars.java` that illustrates how to append the characters in a text string to a `LinkedList` and then display its contents. This code only appends a character that has not already been appended to the array list.

LISTING 6.5: *LinkedListChars.java*

```
import java.util.LinkedList;

public class LinkedListChars
{
    private char chr;
    private int charCount=0;
    private String line = "Line one and line two and three";
    private LinkedList<Character> q1 = new
    LinkedList<Character>();

    public LinkedListChars()
```

```
   {
      // process each character in the current line
      for(int i=0; i<line.length(); i++)
      {
         chr = line.charAt(i);

         // check if character already exists
         boolean found = false;

         for(int j=0; j<q1.size(); j++)
         {
            char ch1 = (Character)q1.get(j);

            if((Character)q1.get(j) == chr) {
               found = true;
               break;
            }
         }

         if(found == false) {
            q1.add(chr);
         }
      }

      System.out.println("Characters: "+q1);
   }

   public static void main (String args[])
   {
      LinkedListChars llc = new LinkedListChars();
   }
}
```

Listing 6.5 defines the class LinkedListChars whose constructor contains a for loop that invokes the charAt() method to initialize the variable chr with a character from the String variable line.

Next, a for loop searches for chr from the contents of the LinkedList q1; if it is not found, then chr is added to q1. This process is repeated for each character of the variable line. Launch the code in Listing 6.5 and you will see the following output:

```
Characters: [L, i, n, e,  , o, a, d, l, t, w, h, r]
```

THE QUEUE CLASS

A Queue is a FIFO (First-In-First-Out) data structure, such as an assembly line in which the first item in that assembly line is the first item that is removed. The Queue class is an interface for which there are multiple implementations, such as ArrayBlockingQueue, LinkedList, PriorityBlockingQueue, PriorityQueue, and SynchronousQueue.

When you create a Queue, you can specify its maximum size. Common operations for a Queue are queue() and dequeue() that append a new element and remove an element, respectively.

When a Queue reaches its capacity, any subsequent additions causes the removal of the oldest (i.e., first) element from the Queue. A Queue is suitable for timeline-related functionality where you want to display entries that were created in chronological order.

Listing 6.6 displays the content of Queue1.java that illustrates how to create a Queue and update its contents.

LISTING 6.6: QueueChars.java

```java
import java.util.LinkedList;
import java.util.Queue;

public class QueueChars
{
    private char chr;
    private int charCount=0;
    private String line = "Line one and line two and three";
    private Queue<Character> q1 = new
    LinkedList<Character>();

    public QueueChars()
    {
        // process each character in the current line
        for(int i=0; i<line.length(); i++)
        {
            chr = line.charAt(i);
            q1.add(chr);
        }

        System.out.println("Characters: "+q1);
    }

    public static void main (String args[])
    {
        QueueChars q1 = new QueueChars();
    }
}
```

Listing 6.6 defines the class QueueChars whose constructor contains a for loop that invokes the charAt() method in order to initialize the variable chr with a character from the String variable line. Next, the character in chr is added to the Queue q1. The output from launching Listing 6.6 is here:

```
Characters: [L, i, n, e,  , o, a, d, l, t, w, h, r]
```

THE TREESET CLASS

As you saw earlier in this chapter, Set is an interface that implemented by the TreeSet class that belongs to the same package. Listing 6.7 displays the content of TreeSet1.java that illustrates how to create a Set and update its contents.

LISTING 6.7: TreeSet1.java

```java
import java.util.Iterator;
import java.util.Set;
import java.util.TreeSet;

public class TreeSet1
{
    private char chr;
    private int charCount=0;
    private String line = "Line one and line two and three";
    private Set<Character> s1 = new TreeSet<Character>();

    public TreeSet1()
    {
        // process each character in the current line
        for(int i=0; i<line.length(); i++)
        {
            chr = line.charAt(i);

            // check if character already exists
            boolean found = false;

            Iterator iter = s1.iterator();
            while (iter.hasNext())
            {
                char chr1 = (Character)iter.next();

                if(chr1 == chr) {
                    found = true;
                    break;
                }
            }

            if(found == false) {
              s1.add(chr);
            }
        }

        System.out.println("Characters: "+s1);
    }

    public static void main (String args[])
    {
        TreeSet1 llc = new TreeSet1();
    }
}
```

Listing 6.7 defines the class TreeSet1 whose constructor contains a for loop that invokes the charAt() method to initialize the variable chr with a character from the String variable line.

Next, a while loop searches for chr in the TreeSet s1; if it is not found, then chr is added to s1. This process is repeated for each character of the variable line. The output from launching Listing 6.7 is here:

```
Characters: [ , L, a, d, e, h, i, l, n, o, r, t, w]
```

THE COLLECTIONS CLASS

The `java.util.Collections` class extends the `Object` class and contains static methods that operate on or return collections. The methods in this class throw a `NullPointerException` if they are given collections or class objects that are null.

Some methods in this class include list-related operations (insert, remove, and so forth) and some arithmetic operations, such as the `min()` method and the `max()` method. Listing 6.8 displays the content of `Collections1.java` that illustrates how to invoke methods in the `Collections` class to update variables defined in the custom `Collections1` class.

LISTING 6.8: Collections1.java

```java
import java.util.ArrayList;
import java.util.Collections;
import java.util.List;

public class Collection1
{
    public static void main(String a[])
    {
        List<String> words1 = new ArrayList<String>();
        words1.add("word1");
        words1.add("word2");

        System.out.println("Initial collection:  "+words1);
        Collections.addAll(words1, "stuffed","pizza");
        System.out.println("Appended collection: "+words1);

        String[] words2 = {"silicon", "valley"};
        Collections.addAll(words1, words2);
        System.out.println("Final collection:    "+words1);
    }
}
```

Listing 6.8 defines the `Collection1` class with a `main()` method that initializes the variable `words1` as an instance of the `ArrayList` class. The next portion of Listing 6.8 appends two words to `words1` and displays the current contents of `words1`. Next, the static method `Collections.addall()` adds two more words to `words1` and displays its contents.

The next code snippet initializes the `String` array `words2` with two strings, after which the static method `Collections.addall()` appends the contents of `words2` to `words1`. The output from launching Listing 6.8 is here:

```
Initial collection:   [word1, word2]
Appended collection:    [word1, word2, stuffed, pizza]
Final collection:       [word1, word2, stuffed, pizza,
                        silicon, valley]
```

Listing 6.9 displays the content of `Collections2.java` that illustrates how to invoke methods in the `Collections` class to update variables defined in the custom `Collections2` class.

LISTING 6.9: Collections2.java

```java
import java.util.ArrayList;
import java.util.Collections;
import java.util.List;

public class Collections2
{
    public static void main(String a[])
    {
        List<Integer> nums = new ArrayList<Integer>();
        nums.add(40);
        nums.add(10);
        nums.add(30);
        nums.add(20);

        int min = Collections.min(nums);
        int max = Collections.max(nums);

        System.out.println("nums:  "+nums);
        System.out.println("Min:   "+min);
        System.out.println("Max:   "+max);

        Collections.sort(nums);
        System.out.println("Sort:  "+nums);
    }
}
```

Listing 6.9 defines the `Collections2` class with a `main()` method that initializes the variable `nums` as an instance of the `ArrayList` class. The next portion of Listing 6.9 calculates the minimum and maximum values in the `nums` list via the methods `min()` and `max()`, respectively, in the `Collections` class.

After displaying the contents of `nums`, the minimum value, and the maximum value, the `sort()` method sorts the elements of `nums`, after which its sorted contents are displayed. The output from launching Listing 6.9 is here:

```
nums:  [40, 10, 30, 20]
Min:   10
Max:   40
Sort:  [10, 20, 30, 40]
```

There are other data structures that you might need for your programming tasks, such as trees, graphs, doubly linked lists, and circular lists. Although Java does not provide built-in classes for these data structures, you can define your own custom classes that implement these data structures.

As a simple illustration, the next section shows you how to define a singly linked list whose elements are instances of a custom Java class.

LINKED LISTS OF OBJECTS

Listing 6.10 displays the contents of the class `Emp` that contains information pertaining to an employee.

LISTING 6.10: Emp.java

```
package com.acme;

public class Emp
{
    public String name, address, id;

    public Emp() {}

    public Emp(String name, String address, String id) {
        this.name    = name;
        this.address = address;
        this.id      = id;
    }

    public static void main(String[] args) {}
}
```

Listing 6.10 defines the class Emp that contains primitive values name, address, and id. This class is simply a value object because there are no other methods in this class, which in turn simplifies the code sample.

Listing 6.11 displays the content of EmpLinkedList.java that illustrates how to create a linked list of elements that are instances of the custom Emp class.

LISTING 6.11: EmpLinkedList.java

```
package com.acme;

import java.util.LinkedList;
import com.acme.Emp;

public class EmpLinkedList
{
    private LinkedList<Emp> empList = new LinkedList<Emp>();

    public void addInitialEmployees()
    {
        System.out.println("*** Initial Employee List ***");
        Emp emp1 = new Emp("Jane Smith", "1234 Main St",
        "1000");
        System.out.println("Adding employee "+emp1.id);
        empList.add(emp1);

        Emp emp2 = new Emp("John Smith", "4321 Oak St",
        "2000");
        System.out.println("Adding employee "+emp2.id);
        empList.add(emp2);

        Emp emp3 = new Emp("Dave Stone", "5678 Maple
        St","3000");
        System.out.println("Adding employee "+emp3.id);
        empList.add(emp3);
        System.out.println("Employee count: "+empList.
        size());
    }
```

```java
public void removeEmployees(int index)
{
    if( empList.size() != 0)
    {
        System.out.println("Removing employee at index
        "+index);
        empList.remove(index);
    }
    else
    {
        System.out.println("Employee list is empty");
    }
}
public void displayEmployees()
{
    System.out.println("*** Current Employee List ***");
    for(int i=0; i<empList.size(); i++)
    {
        Emp emp = (Emp)empList.get(i);
        System.out.println(emp.name+" "+emp.address+"
        "+emp.id);
    }
}
public void findEmployee(String name)
{
    for(int i=0; i<empList.size(); i++)
    {
        Emp emp = (Emp)empList.get(i);
        if(name == emp.name)
        {
            System.out.println("Found employee: "+name);
            return;
        }
    }
    System.out.println("Unknown employee: "+name);
}
public static void main (String args[])
{
    EmpLinkedList llc = new EmpLinkedList();

    llc.addInitialEmployees();
    llc.displayEmployees();
    llc.removeEmployees(1);
    llc.displayEmployees();
    llc.findEmployee("Dave Stone");
    }
}
```

Listing 6.11 defines the class EmpLinkedList that contains instances of the Emp class. Navigate to the parent directory of the com/acme subdirectory and invoke the following command to launch the class EmpLinkedList that belongs to the package com.acme:

```
java com.acme.EmpLinkedList
```

If you need to compile (or recompile) the classes in the `com/acme` subdirectory, you can do so with the following command (from the parent directory of `com/acme`):

```
javac com/acme/*.java
```

After the compilation has completed, you will see the following output:

```
*** Initial Employee List ***
Adding employee 1000
Adding employee 2000
Adding employee 3000
Employee count: 3
*** Current Employee List ***
Jane Smith 1234 Main St 1000
John Smith 4321 Oak St 2000
Dave Stone 5678 Maple St 3000
Removing employee at index 1
*** Current Employee List ***
Jane Smith 1234 Main St 1000
Dave Stone 5678 Maple St 3000
Found employee: Dave Stone
```

GENERIC METHODS

Generic methods enable you to specify one method that can perform the same operation on multiple sets of elements. For example, you can write one generic method for sorting an array of objects, and then invoking the same method with an array of `Integer`, `Double`, or `String` values.

`Generic` methods also provide compile-time checking, which means that you can find invalid data types during the compilation stage. The rules for defining a `Generic` method are listed here:

- A generic method declaration has a type parameter section delimited by angle brackets (< and >) that precedes the return type of the method.
- Each type parameter section contains one or more type parameters (i.e., a generic type name) separated by commas.
- The type parameters can only represent reference types, not primitive types (such as int, double, char, and so forth).
- The type parameters can be used to declare the return type and serve as placeholders for the types of the arguments passed to the generic method.
- The body of a generic method is declared in the same manner as any other method.

Listing 6.12 displays the content of `Generic1.java` that illustrates how to define a generic method that can print arrays that contain different types of values.

LISTING 6.12: Generic1.java

```java
public class Generic1
{
    // generic method printArray
    public static <E> void printArray( E[] inputArray )
    {
        // Display array elements
        for( E element : inputArray )
        {
            System.out.printf( "%s ", element );
        }

        System.out.println();
    }

    public static void main( String args[] )
    {
        // Create arrays of Integer, Double and Character
        Integer[] intArray = { 1, 2, 3, 4, 5 };
        Double[] doubleArray = { 1.1, 2.2, 3.3, 4.4 };
        Character[] charArray = { 'H', 'E', 'L', 'L', 'O'
};

        System.out.println( "Array integerArray contains:"
);

        printArray( intArray ); // pass an Integer array

        System.out.println( "\nArray doubleArray contains:"
);

        printArray( doubleArray ); // pass a Double array

        System.out.println("\nArray characterArray
contains:");
        printArray( charArray ); // pass a Character array
    }
}
```

Listing 6.12 defines the class Generic1 with a public static method called printArray() whose lone parameter takes an array of elements of type E. This method uses a for loop to iterate through the elements of E.

Next, the main() method initializes three arrays: an array of integers, an array of floating point numbers, and an array of characters. The remaining portion of the main() method invokes the printArray() method three times to display the contents of all three arrays. The output from Listing 6.12 is here:

```
Array integerArray contains:
1 2 3 4 5 6

Array doubleArray contains:
1.1 2.2 3.3 4.4

Array characterArray contains:
H E L L O
```

GENERIC CLASSES

A *generic class* includes a type parameter in the definition of the Java class. As with generic methods, the type parameter section of a generic class can have one or more type parameters separated by commas. These classes are known as *parameterized classes* or *parameterized types* because they accept one or more parameters. Listing 6.13 displays the content of Box.java that illustrates how to define a generic class.

LISTING 6.13: Box.java

```java
public class Box<T>
{
  private T t;

  public void add(T t) {
    this.t = t;
  }

  public T get() {
    return t;
  }

  public static void main(String[] args)
  {
    Box<Integer> integerBox = new Box<Integer>();
    Box<String> stringBox = new Box<String>();

    integerBox.add(new Integer(10));
    stringBox.add(new String("Hello World"));

    System.out.printf("Integer Value :%d\n\n", integerBox.
    get());
    System.out.printf("String Value :%s\n", stringBox.get());
  }
}
```

Listing 6.13 defines the class Box and a main() method that creates two instances of the Box class: integerBox of type Integer and stringBox of type String.

Next, the add() method of these two variables is invoked to add an element of type Integer and String, respectively. The last portion of the main() method invokes the get() method to retrieve and then display the values 10 and Hello World that were added in the preceding code block. Launch the preceding code to see the following output:

```
Integer Value :10
String Value :Hello World
```

COUNTING DISTINCT CHARACTERS

Listing 6.14 displays the content of DistinctChars.java that counts the number of distinct characters in a text string.

LISTING 6.14: DistinctChars.java

```java
import java.io.*;
import java.util.Collections;
import java.util.Hashtable;
import java.util.Iterator;
import java.util.List;

public class DistinctChars
{
    private char chr;
    private int charCount=0;
    private String line = "Line one and line two and three";
    private DataInput is;
    private Hashtable ht = new Hashtable();

    public DistinctChars()
    {
        // process each character in the current line
        for(int i=0; i<line.length(); i++)
        {
            chr = line.charAt(i);
            if(ht.get(chr) == null) {
                ht.put(chr, 0);
            }

            charCount = (Integer)ht.get(chr);
            ht.put(chr, ++charCount);
        }
    /*
        for( Iterator iter=ht.keySet().iterator(); iter.
        hasNext(); )
        {
            Character key = (Character) iter.next();
            int value = (Integer) ht.get(key);
            System.out.println("Character: "+key+" Count:
            "+value);
        }
    */
        List<Character> tmp = Collections.list(ht.keys());
        Collections.sort(tmp);
        Iterator<Character> it = tmp.iterator();

        // display ordered items
        while(it.hasNext()){
            char key = it.next();
            int value = (Integer) ht.get(key);
            System.out.println("Character: "+key+" Count:
            "+value);
        }
    }

    public static void main (String args[])
    {
        DistinctChars dc1 = new DistinctChars();
    }
}
```

Listing 6.14 defines the class `DistinctChars` whose constructor contains a `for` loop that invokes the `charAt()` method to initialize the variable `chr` with a character from the `String` variable `line`. If `chr` does not exist in the `Hashtable ht`, then its value is initialized to 0, after which `charCount` is incremented by one. Think about this for a minute to convince yourself that the logic is correct.

Next, a `while` loop iterates through the elements of `ht` and displays their values and their count (i.e., the number of occurrences of each letter). The output from launching Listing 6.14 is here:

```
Character:    Count: 6
Character: L Count: 1
Character: a Count: 2
Character: d Count: 2
Character: e Count: 5
Character: h Count: 1
Character: i Count: 2
Character: l Count: 1
Character: n Count: 5
Character: o Count: 2
Character: r Count: 1
Character: t Count: 2
Character: w Count: 1
```

The preceding list is sorted according to the `ASCII` collating sequence in which uppercase letters precede lowercase letters.

JAVA 8 ENHANCEMENTS FOR COLLECTIONS

Java 8 uses both lambda expressions as well as default methods to improve the Collection framework that is available in earlier versions of Java. Now would be a good time to read about these two topics, discussed earlier in this chapter, if you have not already done so.

Some of the new methods in the `java.lang.Iterable` package are here:

- `default void forEach(consumer<? Super T>action)`
- `default Spliterator<T> spliterator()`

Some of the new methods in the `java.util.Collection` package are here:

- `default Boolean removeIf(Predicate<? Super E>filter)`
- `default Spliterator<E> spliterator()`
- `default Stream<E> stream()`
- `default Stream<E> parallelStream()`

Finally, the Java 8 `java.util.Map` package also contains numerous new methods:

- `default V getOrDefault(Object key, V defaultValue)`
- `putIfAbsent(K key, V value)`

SUMMARY

In this chapter, you learned about some of the legacy classes in `Java`, along with an introduction to `Iterators` and how they are used in different versions of `Java`. Next you learned about some of the most common `Collection` interfaces and classes, followed by code samples that use the `Collection` framework.

In addition, you learned how to find the distinct characters using a method in the `Collection` classes. Lastly, you learned about some of the useful methods in the `Java` 8 enhancement for the `Collection` classes.

CHAPTER 7

STREAMS AND FILES

This chapter introduces you to Java streams, which enable you to perform various tasks, such as read characters from the console, read data from files and write data to files, and handle streams of data coming from Web services or other data sources.

The first part of this chapter provides a quick overview of streams and some stream-oriented classes. You will see code samples that use some of these classes to read input from the console. After reading these code samples, compare them with the code samples for reading user input in Chapter 1.

The second part of this chapter involves file-oriented classes for reading files, such as the `FileInputStream`, `FilterInputStream`, `BufferedInputStream`, and `DataInputStream` classes. You will learn how to read characters from the console and how to read line-oriented user input with these classes. This section also shows you how to count words and characters in a file and how to search for a string in a file.

The third part of this chapter involves file-oriented classes for writing data to files, such as the `FileWriter` and `BufferedWriter` classes. This section also shows you how to list the files in a directory, and then you will learn about serialization and deserialization of data.

WORKING WITH STREAMS IN JAVA

A *stream* is a high-level concept that refers to a source of data or a destination for data. The specific types of sources and destinations are implemented via lower level classes. For example, the notion of a file can be a physical file on your disk (for read/write operations), or an output file can be a printer. Streams and files have one thing in common: either you are getting data from some location, or you are sending (writing) data to a location, or both.

With the preceding observation in mind, Java input streams read data from a stream whereas Java output streams write data to a stream. Java provides the package java.io with stream-related classes that contain methods for manipulating text files and binary files. The java.io package contains more than 50 classes that serve as readers, writers, input streams, and output streams. Some of the stream-related classes include the following:

- BufferedOutputStream
- ByteArrayOutputStream
- DataOutputStream
- FileOutputStream
- FilterOutputStream
- InputStream
- ObjectOutputStream
- OutputStream
- PipedOutputStream
- OutputStreamWriter
- PipedInputStream

Most of these output streams have corresponding input streams in the java.io package. Stream operations can obviously encounter errors, which are handled by the classes Exception, FileNotFoundException, and IOException.

The abstract classes InputStream and OutputStream are the top-level classes of the byte stream hierarchy, and both of them throw an IOException when an error occurs. For example, you can read user input via System.in, which is actually a subclass of InputStream that contains three versions of the read() method. These three versions read a byte stream, and they return -1 when the end of a stream is encountered.

However, consider using a buffered class for input or for output instead of its corresponding non-buffered class to improve performance. For example, the class BufferedInputStream has a constructor that takes an InputStream as a parameter; similarly, the BufferedOutputStream has a constructor that takes an OutputStream as a parameter.

As a specific example, whenever you write data to a file on your disk or you read data from a file on your disk, you can be assured that these operations involve buffered input and output. Word processors also work in this fashion. You can search online for the full list of methods that are available for the classes in the java.io package.

Another key point: when you invoke methods in the classes in the java.io package, you typically place them inside a try/catch/finally block to handle file-related exceptions (perhaps the file does not exist, or it's in a different location). In addition, you want to ensure that streams are closed and resources are properly deallocated (otherwise you will have memory leaks in your applications).

There are also interfaces in the `java.io`, such as `DataInput` and `DataOutput`. Recall that the preferred practice is to specify interfaces (rather than concrete objects or primitive types) as parameters for methods, and also when you instantiate objects. The reason for doing so is that you pass *any* instance of a class that (directly or indirectly) implements the specified interface. Keep this point in mind when you see examples in this chapter that use the `DataInput` and `DataOutput` interfaces of the `java.io` package.

As mentioned earlier, the `java.io` package contains two abstract Java classes `InputStream` and `OutputStream` that are the base classes for the other stream-oriented classes, and they are discussed in the next section.

THE ABSTRACT CLASS INPUTSTREAM

As you learned in the previous section, `InputStream` is an abstract class, and every method in `InputStream`-based classes throws a `java.io.IOException`, which in turn is a subclass of the `Exception` class. The `InputStream` classes provide a `read()` method (along with its variants) to read data from an input stream. Since the `read()` method also waits until data is available, the `read()` method is a "blocking" method.

When an application makes an API call and "waits" for the result, the application is invoking a synchronous operation. If the application does not wait for the result, then the API is an asynchronous API, and typically the API specifies a "callback" function to invoke when the result is returned to the application.

In the case of input and output streams, you are responsible for closing those streams after you have finished using them. In general, you close an input stream in a `catch` block in the case of an error, and then in the `finally` block during normal code execution.

THE FILEINPUTSTREAM CLASS

The `FileInputStream` class can be used to read data from a file on the file system, as shown in this code snippet:

```
InputStream is = new FileInputStream("/path/and/fileName");
```

Notice that the left side of the preceding code snippet specifies `InputStream`, whereas the right side specifies the `FileInputStream` class. The reason this code works is because `FileInputStream` is a subclass of `InputStream` (which is an abstract class).

Recall from Chapter 4 that if B is a subclass of A, then occurrences of A can be replaced with occurrences of B, so both of the following code snippets are valid:

```
A a1 = new A();
A a2 = new B();
```

Another way to perform a similar read operation is with the following code snippet:

```
FileInputStream fis = new FileInputStream("/path/and/
fileName");
```

One other point to remember is that the implementation of the method `finalize()` in `FileInputStream` (which is a *protected* method) will close the stream, and therefore you do not need to explicitly close that stream in your code.

In many cases, the garbage collector invokes the `finalize()` method when a stream is no longer in use (but you don't know when the stream is actually closed). Due to a time delay, you need to be careful not to write content to files, close the files, and then open them again too quickly, because doing so could result in an inconsistent state. You can also consider invoking the `close()` method if you are not sure of the exact type of `InputStream` that you received in your method.

THE FILTERINPUTSTREAM CLASS

The `FilterInputStream` class is an abstract class that essentially acts as a "pass along" gate for the methods in the `InputStream` interface. An interesting fact about the `FilterInputStream` class is that you can make multiple nested invocations, as shown here:

```
InputStream         is1 = getAnInputStream();
FilterInputStream   fis1 = new FilterInputStream(is1);
FilterInputStream   fis2 = new FilterInputStream(fis1);
FilterInputStream   fis3 = new FilterInputStream(fis2);
```

After a read operation is performed in `fis3`, the request is sent to `fis2`, which forwards the request to `fis1`, until `fis1` provides some data. The preceding construct can also be implemented via method chaining, as well as using this technique:

```
fis3 = new FilterInputStream(new
            FilterInputStream(new FilterInputStream(is1)));
```

The preceding construct is simple and clear and also recommended instead of the other alternatives. The next several sections contain information about some of the subclasses of `FilterInputStream`.

THE BUFFEREDINPUTSTREAM CLASS

The `BufferedInputStream` class implements the methods in `InputStream`. In addition, the `BufferedInputStream` class handles larger blocks of data more efficiently (as you would expect from a buffered class). If need be, you can perform different "wrapping" operations, such as the following code snippet:

```
InputStream is = new BufferedInputStream(new
FileInputStream("a.txt"));
```

The preceding code snippet creates a buffered input stream from the file a.txt, which enables you to take advantage of the buffered nature of the stream.

THE DATAINPUTSTREAM CLASS

The DataInputStream class implements the DataInput interface that in turn contains a high-level set of methods (all of which throw an IOException) that work well with more complex streams.

Some of the methods include readFully(), skipBytes(), readBoolean(), readByte(), and readDataType(), where you can replace DataType with Char, Int, Long, Float, and Double.

The following code block contains an example of the DataInputStream class:

```
DataInputStream dis = new DataInputStream(getNumericInput
                     Stream());
long size = s.readLong(); // the number of items in the stream
while (size-- > 0) {
    if (s.readBoolean()) {    // process this item
        int     anInteger    = s.readInt();
        int     magicBitFlags = s.readUnsignedShort();
        double  aDouble      = s.readDouble();

        if ((magicBitFlags & 0100000) != 0) {
          // high bit set, do something special
        }
        // process anInteger and aDouble
    }
}
```

Many of the methods in DataInputStream throw an EOFException when the end of a stream is reached.

READING USER INPUT FROM THE CONSOLE

Java code for reading input from the console involves reading from the System.in class. Note that the appropriate code block involves "wrapping" System.in inside a BufferedReader object to create a character stream: after doing so, you can then use read() to read a character or readLine() to read a string. The code for the preceding sentence is illustrated in the following code snippet:

```
BufferedReader br = new BufferedReader(
                    new InputStreamReader(System.in));
```

The next section contains a complete code sample for reading line-oriented user input.

Reading Line-Oriented User Input

Listing 7.1 displays the content of ReadUserInput1.java that "wraps" a DataInputStream class around System.in() in order to read user input from the command line, and then displays each line of user input.

LISTING 7.1: ReadUserInput1.java

```java
import java.io.DataInput;
import java.io.DataInputStream;
import java.io.IOException;

public class ReadUserInput1
{
    public static void main(String args[])
    {
        char chr;
        String line;

        DataInput dis = new DataInputStream(System.in);

        try {
            for(;;)
            {
                line = dis.readLine();
                if(line != null && line.length() > 0) {
                    String trim = line.trim();
                    System.out.println("Original: x"+line+"x");
                    System.out.println("Trimmed:  x"+trim+"x");
                }
                else {
                    break;
                }
            }
        }
        catch (IOException ioe) { }
    }
}
```

Listing 7.1 defines the `ReadUserInput` class whose `main()` method initializes the variable `dis` as an instance of the `DataInputStream` that "wraps" the standard input `System.in`.

The next portion of Listing 7.1 is a `try/catch` block that contains a `for` loop that executes "forever" (i.e., until there is no additional user input from the command line). This loop reads a user-provided input line and trims the outer white spaces. The next portion prepends and appends the character `x` to the original line and the trimmed line, and then prints the result. A sample output from Listing 7.1 is here:

```
Original: xqwerx
Trimmed:  xqwerx
  asdf
Original: x  asdf  x
Trimmed:  xasdfx
```

READING CHARACTER-ORIENTED USER INPUT

Listing 7.2 displays the content of `BufferedRead.java` that reads user input from the command line, and then displays each line of user input.

LISTING 7.2: BufferedRead.java

```java
import java.io.BufferedReader;
import java.io.InputStreamReader;
import java.io.IOException;

public class BufferedRead
{
    public static void main(String args[]) throws
    IOException
    {
        char chr;

        // Create a BufferedReader using System.in
        BufferedReader br = new BufferedReader(new
                        InputStreamReader(System.in));
        System.out.println("Enter characters or 'x' to
        exit");

        // read characters
        do {
            chr = (char) br.read();
            if(chr != '\n')
            {
                System.out.println("char: "+chr);
            }
        } while(chr != 'x');
    }
}
```

Listing 7.2 defines the class `BufferedRead` and a `main()` method that initializes the variable `br` as an instance of a `BufferedReader` class that wraps the `InputStreamReader` class, which in turn wraps `System.in`. A sample output from Listing 7.2 is here:

```
Enter characters or 'x' to exit
asd
char: a
char: s
char: d
qex
char: q
char: e
char: x
```

READING A TEXT FILE

Listing 7.3 displays the content of `ReadTextFile1.java` that opens a text file and reads its contents.

LISTING 7.3: ReadTextFile1.java

```java
import java.io.*;
class ReadTextFile1
```

```
{
    private String inFile = "text1.txt";
    private String line;
    //private DataInput is;

    public ReadTextFile1()
    {
        try {
            // NB: declare is outside the try block to
            // make it available in the finally block
            DataInput is =
                new DataInputStream(new
                FileInputStream(inFile));

            while ((line = is.readLine()) != null)
            {
                System.out.println("Line: "+line);
            }
        }
        catch (IOException ioe) {
            ioe.printStackTrace();
        }
        finally {
            // fails because 'is' is defined in 'try':
            //is.close();
        }
    }

    public static void main (String args[])
    {
        ReadTextFile1 rtf1 = new ReadTextFile1();
    }
}
```

Listing 7.3 defines the class ReadTextFile1 and a main() method that contains a try/catch/finally code block. Inside the try block is the variable is, which is an instance of the DataInputStream class that wraps a FileInputStream around an input file called text1.txt.

The next portion of the code contains a while loop that reads the contents of text1.txt in a line-by-line fashion, and then prints each input line. The catch block is invoked in case there is an error (such as a missing file).

The finally code block does *not* close the input stream is (which is currently commented out in the code), as noted in the comment statement. To close the input stream in the finally block, you must declare the is variable *outside* the try code block so that it will be accessible in the finally block:

```
DataInputStream is = null;
try {
 // same code
}
catch (IOException ioe) {
    ioe.printStackTrace();
}
```

```
finally {
    is.close();
}
```

Launch the code in Listing 7.3 and you will see the following output:

```
Line: line one
Line: line two
Line: line three
```

The contents of `file.txt` are shown below:

```
line one
line two
line three
```

READING A CSV FILE

There are two ways that you read the contents of a CSV file using Java code. One way is to use the `StringTokenizer` class that enables you to tokenize a line of text using the default delimiter (" ") or by specifying some other character, such as a comma or pipe ("|") symbol.

Another technique involves the `split()` method that uses a regular expression.

Although the `StringTokenizer` class is retained for compatibility reasons, the `split()` method or the `java.util.regex` package is recommended. One advantage of the `String.split()` method is its support for *multiple* delimiters because it is based on regular expressions, whereas `StringTokenizer` can only specify a *single* delimiter.

Listing 7.4 displays the content of `ReadCSV1.java` that reads the names in a text file in a line-oriented fashion.

LISTING 7.4: ReadCSV1.java

```java
import java.io.*;

import java.util.StringTokenizer;

public class ReadCSV1
{
    private String line, fname, lname;
    private String inFile = "names1.txt";
    private String delim = ",";
    private DataInput is;

    public ReadCSV1()
    {
        try {
            is = new DataInputStream(new
FileInputStream(inFile));

            while ((line = is.readLine()) != null)
```

```
      {
          if(line.startsWith("#"))
          {
           // skip comment line
          }
          else
          {
           //using the StringTokenizer class:
              StringTokenizer st = new
              StringTokenizer(line,delim);
              fname = (String)st.nextElement();
              lname = (String)st.nextElement();
              System.out.println("My name is "+fname+"
              "+lname);

           //using the split() method to tokenize:
           //String[] person = line.split(delim);
           //System.out.println("My name is "+
           //                    person[0]+" "+person[1]);
          }
      }
    }
    catch (IOException ioe) {
      ioe.printStackTrace();
    }
    finally {
     //is.close();
    }
  }

  public static void main (String args[])
  {
      ReadCSV1 rtf1 = new ReadCSV1();
  }
}
```

Listing 7.4 defines the class ReadCSV1 that contains a main() method and a constructor that contains a try/catch/finally block. The try block contains a while loop that reads the contents of the file names1.txt on a line-by-line basis.

If the first character of a line of text is the # character, then this line is ignored; i.e., it's treated as a comment line. Otherwise, that text line is split into tokens (words) via an instance st of the StringTokenizer class. The fname and lname variables are initialized by successive invocations of the nextToken() method, and then the person's name is printed, using this code snippet:

```
System.out.println("My name is "+fname+" "+lname);
```

The last portion of the main() method contains a catch block that catches errors and a finally block that closes the input file stream. Launch the code in Listing 7.4 and you will see the following output:

```
My name is Jane Smith
My name is John Jones
My name is Bob Stone
```

Listing 7.5 displays the content of `names1.txt` that is referenced in Listing 7.4.

LISTING 7.5: names1.txt

```
#first name and last name
Jane,Smith
John,Jones
Bob,Stone
```

If you decide to use the `split()` method, you can match the fields in a line of text against multiple delimiters using the following type of code snippet that checks three characters as delimiters:

```
String[] person = line.split(",|;");
```

WRITING DATA TO A TEXT FILE

Listing 7.6 displays the content of `WriteTextFile1.java` that reads the contents of one text file and then creates a new file with the same contents, thereby simulating a copy command.

LISTING 7.6: WriteTextFile1.java

```java
import java.io.*;

class WriteTextFile1
{
   private String line;
   private String inFile  = "text1.txt";
   private String outFile = "text1copy.txt";
   private DataInput is;
   private DataOutput os;

   public WriteTextFile1()
   {
      try {
         is = new DataInputStream(new
         FileInputStream(inFile));
         os = new DataOutputStream(new
         FileOutputStream(outFile));

         while ((line = is.readLine()) != null)
         {
            StringBuffer modifiedLine = new
            StringBuffer(line);
            os.writeBytes(modifiedLine.toString()+"\n");
         }
      }
      catch (IOException ioe) {
        ioe.printStackTrace();
      }
      finally {
       //is.close();
```

```
        //os.close();
    }
}

public static void main (String args[])
{
    WriteTextFile1 rtf1 = new WriteTextFile1();
}
}
```

Listing 7.6 creates the class `WriteTextFile1` and contains a `main()` method that copies the contents of `text1.txt` to the file `text1copy.txt`. The code to read the contents of `text1.txt` is the same as the code in Listing 7.5.

The code to write to the new destination involves defining an output stream that wraps the file `text1copy.txt`, as shown here:

```
os = new DataOutputStream(new FileOutputStream(outFile));
```

The `try` code block contains a loop that reads the contents of `text1.txt` on a line-by-line basis, and then writes each line to the output file, as shown here:

```
while ((line = is.readLine()) != null)
{
    StringBuffer modifiedLine = new StringBuffer(line);
    os.writeBytes(modifiedLine.toString()+"\n");
}
```

The `catch` block and the `finally` block contain code that you have already seen in earlier examples. Launch the code in Listing 7.6 and you will see a new file on the file system whose contents are identical to the file `text1.txt`.

The FileWriter Class

The Java `FileWriter` class is more low level than the `PrintWriter` class (discussed in the next section) in the sense that it writes only strings and char arrays. If you pass a variable of type `File` to the `FileWriter` class, it opens the file in an unbuffered manner, whereas the `PrintWriter` class does so in a buffered fashion. While `PrintWriter` does not throw `IOExceptions`, the `FileWriter` class throws `IOException` in case of any IO failure.

The `write()` method in the `FileWriter` class overwrites the contents of a file, whereas the `append()` method in the `FileWriter` class appends data to a file (which is probably what you expected).

Listing 7.7 displays the content of `AppendToFile.java` that writes a line of text to a file using the `write()` method, followed by appending a second line of text to a file using the `append()` method.

LISTING 7.7: AppendToFile.java

```
import java.io.IOException;
import java.io.FileWriter;
```

```
class AppendToFile
{
    public static void main(String[] args) throws IOException
    {
        FileWriter file = null;

        try {
            file = new FileWriter("twolines.txt");
            file.write("The first line\n");
            file.append("The second line\n");
        } catch(IOException ioe) {
            System.out.println("Write failed: throwing an
            exception");
            throw ioe;
        } finally {
            file.close();
        }
    }
}
```

Listing 7.7 starts with two import statements and then the declaration of the AppendToFile class, followed by a main() method that contains a try/catch block to write data to a text file.

The variable file is initialized as an instance of the FileWriter class that will write two lines of text to the file twolines.txt by invoking the write() method for the first line and then invoking the append() method for the second line.

If an error occurs, the catch block displays a message, otherwise the finally block closes the output file. Launch the code in Listing 7.7 to see the contents of the file twolines.txt, as shown here:

```
The first line
The second line
```

The PrintWriter Class

The PrintWriter class extends the Writer class, and also implements all the print methods found in PrintStream, but it does not handle raw bytes. This class supports automatic flushing that is performed when the println() or print() methods are invoked. Hence, flushing is not based on a newline character in the output stream.

Moreover, the PrintWriter class methods do not throw I/O exceptions: they set a Boolean flag that can be accessed via the checkError() method.

The PrintStream Class

The PrintStream class extends the FilterWriterStream class and allows you to write formatted data as text to an underlying OutputStream instead of their byte values.

All characters printed by a PrintStream are converted into bytes using the default character encoding of the underlying platform. Note that the PrintWriter class is preferred in situations that involve writing characters rather than bytes.

In addition, the `PrintStream` class methods do not throw I/O exceptions: they set a Boolean flag that can be accessed via the `checkError()` method (just like the `PrintWriter` class).

COUNTING WORDS AND CHARACTERS IN A FILE

Listing 7.8 displays the content of `WordsAndChars.java` that counts the number of words and characters in the text file `Words.txt`, whose contents are shown in Listing 7.9.

LISTING 7.8: WordsAndChars.java

```
import java.io.*;

public class WordsAndChars
{
    private int wordCount=0, charCount=0;
    private String line, word, delim = " ";
    private String inFile = "Words.txt";
    private DataInput is;

    public WordsAndChars()
    {
        try {
            is = new DataInputStream(new
            FileInputStream(inFile));

            while((line = is.readLine()) != null)
            {
                String[] words = line.trim().split("\\w+");

                // process each word in the current line
                for(int i=0; i<words.length; i++)
                {
                    ++wordCount;
                    charCount += words[i].length();
                }
            }
        }
        catch (IOException ioe) {
            ioe.printStackTrace();
        }
        finally {
         //is.close();
        }

        System.out.println("Word Count: "+wordCount);
        System.out.println("Char Count: "+charCount);
    }

    public static void main (String args[])
    {
        WordsAndChars rtf1 = new WordsAndChars();
    }
}
```

Listing 7.8 defines the class WordsAndChars, which has a constructor that contains a try/catch/finally code block. The try block contains a while loop that reads and tokenizes the contents of the file Words.txt on a line-by-line basis.

Next, a for loop counts the number of words (tokens) in the current tokenized line, and then updates the total character count. Note that the character count does not take into account the spaces between the words in the text file Words.txt. The last portion of the main() method contains a catch() block and a finally() block that contains the usual functionality. The output from Listing 7.8 is here:

```
Word Count: 11
Char Count: 43
```

Listing 7.9 displays the content of Words.txt that is used in Listing 7.8.

LISTING 7.9: Words.txt

```
First line of text
Second line of text
The third line
```

The next section of this chapter shows you how to perform search operations in text files.

SEARCH FOR A STRING IN A FILE

Listing 7.10 displays the content of SearchWord.java that illustrates how to search for a string in a text file.

LISTING 7.10: SearchWord.java

```java
import java.io.*;

public class SearchWord
{
    private int wordCount=0;
    private String search="line", delim = " ";
    private String line, inFile = "Words.txt";
    private DataInput is;

    public SearchWord()
    {
        try {
            is = new DataInputStream(new
            FileInputStream(inFile));

            while((line = is.readLine()) != null)
            {
                String[] words = line.trim().split(" ");

                // process each word in the current line
```

```
            for(int i=0; i<words.length; i++)
            {
                if(words[i].equalsIgnoreCase(search))
                {
                    ++wordCount;
                }
            }
        }

        System.out.println("Search Word: "+search);
        System.out.println("Word Count:  "+wordCount);
    }
    catch (IOException ioe) {
      ioe.printStackTrace();
    }
    finally {
      //is.close();
    }
  }

  public static void main (String args[])
  {
      SearchWord rtf1 = new SearchWord();
  }
}
```

Listing 7.10 defines the class `SearchWorld` and a `main()` method that contains a `try/catch/finally` block. The `try` block contains a `while` loop that reads the contents of `Words.txt` on a line-by-line basis.

Each line is trimmed of leading and trailing white spaces and then tokenized by the `split()` function. The next portion of the `try` block contains a `for` loop that does a case-insensitive comparison of each token with the word "line." If a match occurs, then the `wordCount` is incremented. The last portion of the `try` block displays the search word and the number of (case-insensitive) matches.

The last portion of the `main()` method contains a `catch()` block and a `finally()` block that contain the usual functionality. The output from Listing 7.10 is here:

```
Search Word: line
Word Count:  3
```

THE BUFFEREDWRITER CLASS

Listing 7.11 displays the content of `BufferedWriterExample.java` that illustrates how to write a line of text to a file using the `write()` method, and then appends a second line of text to a file using the `append()` method.

LISTING 7.11: BufferedWriterExample.java

```
import java.io.IOException;
import java.io.BufferedWriter;
import java.io.File;
```

```
import java.io.FileWriter;
import java.io.IOException;

public class BufferedWriterExample
{
    public static void main(String[] args)
    {
        String line1 = "The first line\n";
        String line2 = "The second line\n";

        try {
            File file = new File("bufferedwriter.txt");
            FileWriter fw = new FileWriter(file);
            BufferedWriter bw = new BufferedWriter(fw);

            bw.write(line1);
            bw.append(line2);
            bw.close();
        }
        catch (IOException e) {
            e.printStackTrace();
        }
    }
}
```

Listing 7.11 contains various `import` statements and the `main()` method that initializes the string variables `line1` and `line2` as a text string. The next portion of Listing 7.11 consists of a `try/catch` block that defines the variable `bw` as an instance of the `BufferedWriter` class, which involves writing text to the output file called `bufferedwriter.txt`. In this example, the contents of `line1` and `line2` are written to the output file. Launch the code in Listing 7.11 and then display the contents of the file `bufferedwriter.txt`, as shown here:

```
The first line
The second line
```

The BufferedWriter Class with try-with-resources (Java 7+)

There is a file (that is available for this book) that contains BufferedWriterExample.java that illustrates how to use the `try-with-resources` feature, which is available from `Java` 7 and above. The primary difference is the following replacement for the `try` keyword:

```
try (BufferedWriter bw = new BufferedWriter(new
FileWriter("bw2.txt")))
{
    bw.write(line1);
    bw.write(line2);
    //bw.close(); // no longer necessary
}
```

The benefit of using the preceding syntax is that the file is *automatically closed* after the code has executed, which means that you do not need to explicitly include the code snippet `bw2.close();` in order to close the file.

WORKING WITH DIRECTORIES

Java provides two methods for creating directories: the `mkdir()` method and the `mkdirs()` method. The `mkdir()` method creates a directory, and then returns `true` if the directory was successfully created, and `false` otherwise. Directory creation can fail for various reasons:

- the directory already exists
- intermediate directories do not exist
- insufficient file permissions
- the file path belongs to another user (such as root)

Fortunately, the `mkdirs()` method creates both a directory and all the intermediate directories, which handles the second case in the previous bullet list.

Listing 7.12 displays the content of the file `CreateDir.java` that creates the directory `/tmp/user/java/bin`.

LISTING 7.12: CreateDir.java

```java
import java.io.*;
import java.io.File;

public class CreateDir
{
    public static void main(String args[])
    {
        String newdir = "/tmp/user/java/bin";
        File dir = new File(newdir);

        // Create directory:
        boolean result = dir.mkdirs();
        System.out.println("result: "+result);
    }
}
```

Listing 7.12 defines the class `CreateDir` and a `main()` method that specifies a directory that is several layers below `/tmp`. Since those directories might not exist, the `main()` method invokes the `mkdirs()` method. Note that if you invoke this code multiple times, you will get an error because the directory already exists.

Listing 7.13 displays the content of `ListDirectory.java` that shows the contents of the directory `/tmp`.

LISTING 7.13: ListDirectory.java

```java
import java.io.File;

public class ListDirectory
{
    public static void main(String args[])
    {
        String dirname = "/tmp";
        File file = new File(dirname);
```

```
    if (file.isDirectory())
    {
        System.out.println("Directory of " + dirname);
        String s[] = file.list();

        for (int i=0; i < s.length; i++) {
            File f = new File(dirname+"/" + s[i]);

            if (f.isDirectory())
            {
                System.out.println(s[i]+" is a directory");
            }
            else
            {
                System.out.println(s[i]+" is a file");
            }
        }
    }
    else
    {
        System.out.println(dirname+" is not a directory");
    }
  }
}
```

Listing 7.13 defines the class ListDirectory and the main() method that contains a loop that iterates through the contents of the /tmp directory. A message is displayed depending on whether the current file is a directory or an actual file.

SERIALIZATION

Java supports the concept of serialization, which enables you to convert an object into a byte stream so that you can send the object over a network or store the object on a disk. If you want to support serialization in a custom Java class, then that class must implement the Serializable interface. Note that a serialized object in Java does not contain code.

Java serialization is performed via reflection in order to obtain the data from the fields (including private and final) in a given object that you want to serialize. Moreover, if a given field contains an object, Java will recursively perform serialization on that object.

The ObjectOutputStream class is used to serialize an object. Listing 7.14 displays the content of Employee.java that will be serialized and then deserialized by two other classes.

LISTING 7.14: Employee.java

```
public class Employee implements java.io.Serializable
{
    public String name;
    public String address;
    public transient int SSN;
    public int number;
```

```
public void mailCheck()
{
    System.out.println("Mailing a check to " + name
                            + " " + address);
}
}
```

Listing 7.14 defines the class `Employee` that implements the interface `java.io.Serializable`. Note that this interface does not contain any methods and acts more like a "marker" to indicate that a class is serializable.

Listing 7.15 displays the content of `Serialize.java` that instantiates an `Employee` object and serializes it to a file called `employee.ser`, which is the only "output" of this program.

Note: When serializing an object to a file, the standard convention in Java is to give the file a `ser` extension.

LISTING 7.15: Serialize.java

```
import java.io.*;

public class Serialize
{
    private static String serFile = "/tmp/employee.ser";

    public static void main(String [] args)
    {
        Employee e = new Employee();
        e.name = "John Doe";
        e.address = "1234 Appian Way, San Francisco";
        e.SSN = 123456789;
        e.number = 5000;

        try {
            FileOutputStream fileOut = new
            FileOutputStream(serFile);
            ObjectOutputStream out = new
            ObjectOutputStream(fileOut);
            out.writeObject(e);
            out.close();
            fileOut.close();
            System.out.printf("Serialized data is saved in
            "+serFile);
        }
        catch(IOException i) {
            i.printStackTrace();
        }
    }
}
```

Listing 7.15 defines the class `Serialize` and a `main()` method that consists of two parts. The first part creates an instance of an `Employee` class and populates the name, address, SSN, and number fields.

The second part of the `main()` method contains a `try/catch` code block that attempts to write the serialized version of the `Employee` instance (in the previous code block) to the file location specified by the variable `serFile`. The last portion of the `main()` method is a `catch` block that handles exceptions.

DESERIALIZATION

As you might have already surmised, deserialization is the opposite process of serialization: it recreates an object from a (serialized) byte stream.

Listing 7.16 displays the content of the file `Deserialize.java` that illustrates how to deserialize the `Employee` object that was created in the `Serialize` program.

LISTING 7.16: Deserialize.java

```java
import java.io.*;

public class Deserialize
{
  private static String serFile = "/tmp/employee.ser";

  public static void main(String [] args)
  {
     Employee object1 = null;

     try {
         // Read the object from a file:
         FileInputStream file = new
         FileInputStream(serFile);
         ObjectInputStream in = new ObjectInputStream(file);

         // deserialization of object:
         object1 = (Employee)in.readObject();

         in.close();
         file.close();

         System.out.println("name =    " + object1.name);
         System.out.println("address = " + object1.
         address);
         System.out.println("SSN =    " + object1.SSN);
         System.out.println("number = " + object1.number);
     } catch(IOException ex) {
         System.out.println("IOException occurred");
     } catch(ClassNotFoundException ex) {
         System.out.println("ClassNotFoundException");
     }
  }
}
```

The code in Listing 7.16 performs the opposite of Listing 7.15: a serialized file on the file system is read into a variable that is then reconstituted into an instance of the `Employee` class.

Listing 7.16 contains a `main()` routine with a `try/catch` block that handles a `ClassNotFoundException`, which is declared by the `readObject()`

method. In order for the JVM (Java Virtual Machine) to deserialize an object, it must be able to find the byte code for the class; otherwise, the JVM throws a ClassNotFoundException. Also notice that the return value of readObject() is cast to an Employee reference.

The value of the SSN field was 123456789 when the object was serialized, but since the field is transient, this value was *not* sent to the output stream. The SSN field of the deserialized Employee object is 0. The output from Listing 7.16 is here:

```
name =    John Doe
address = 1234 Appian Way, San Francisco
SSN =     0
number =  5000
```

REFLECTION

Reflection in Java is a very powerful feature that enables the program to introspect itself to manipulate internal properties of the program, such a finding the names of its members.

Listing 7.17 displays the content of the file ShowMymethods.java that illustrates how to display the names of the methods in the ShowMymethods class.

LISTING 7.17: ShowMyMethods.java

```java
import java.lang.reflect.*;

public class ShowMyMethods
{
    public void emptyMethod1(){}
    public void emptyMethod2(){}
    public void emptyMethod3(){}

    public static void main(String args[])
    {
        try {
            //Class clz = Class.forName(args[0]);
            Class clz = Class.forName("ShowMyMethods");
            Method m[] = clz.getDeclaredMethods();

            for (int i = 0; i < m.length; i++)
            {
                System.out.println("method: "+m[i].toString());
            }
        }
        catch (Throwable e) {
            System.err.println(e);
        }
    }
}
```

Listing 7.17 starts with an import statement for the reflection-related classes, followed by the declaration of the ShowMyMethods class that defines three empty methods.

Next, the `main()` method contains a `try/catch` block to initialize the variable `clz` and then obtain an array m of the methods in the class `ShowMyMethods`. The final portion of the `main()` method contains a loop that iterates through the array m and displays its contents. Launch the code in Listing 7.17 and you will see the following output:

```
method: public void ShowMyMethods.emptyMethod1()
method: public void ShowMyMethods.emptyMethod2()
method: public void ShowMyMethods.emptyMethod3()
method: public static void ShowMyMethods.main(java.lang.
String[])
```

As you can see, Listing 7.17 contains the following commented out code snippet:

```
//Class clz = Class.forName(args[0]);
```

You can uncomment the preceding code snippet to perform reflection on a class that you specify from the command line, an example of which is shown here:

```
java ShowMyMethods AnotherJavaClass
```

Despite this extremely brief introduction, you can probably appreciate the usefulness of reflection that is also used in Java class loaders, which is another interesting (and more advanced) topic. Perform an online search for more detailed information regarding Java reflection and class loaders.

ANNOTATIONS

Java annotations provide information to the compiler. For instance, Java provides an `@override` annotation that you can use (by specifying `@override` before a method) to indicate that the annotated method is overriding a method with the same name.

Java also supports `@Deprecated` and `@SuppressWarnings` to mark a method as deprecated and to suppress warning messages, respectively. Annotations reduce the amount of boilerplate code that you need to write manually. In addition, annotations can provide compile-time information to the compiler that other tools can process accordingly.

Listing 7.18 displays the content of `MyAnnotation.java` that illustrates how to use a Java annotation.

LISTING 7.18: MyAnnotation.java

```
class ClassA
{
    public ClassA()
    {
        this.simpleMethod();
    }
```

```
    public void simpleMethod()
    {
        System.out.println("Inside simpleMethod in classA");
    }
}
public class MyAnnotation extends ClassA
{
    public MyAnnotation()
    {
        super();
    }

    @Override
    public void simpleMethod()
    {
        System.out.println("Inside simpleMethod in
        MyAnnotation");
    }

    public static void main(String args[])
    {
        MyAnnotation ma = new MyAnnotation();
        ma.simpleMethod();
    }
}
```

Listing 7.18 defines the inner class ClassA and the class MyAnnotation that extends ClassA: both classes contain the method simpleMethod(), which is overridden in MyAnnotation.

Listing 7.18 also defines a main() method that initializes the variable ma as an instance of MyAnnotation, and then invokes simpleMethod(). Notice the cascading sequence of events: the constructor for MyAnnotation invokes the constructor of ClassA by invoking super() in the constructor of the latter. Next, the constructor of ClassA invokes simpleMethod(), which displays the message specified in simpleMethod() that belongs to MyAnnotation, and *not* the simpleMethod() code in ClassA.

In addition, the constructor for MyAnnotation invokes simpleMethod(), which means that the same text string is displayed twice. Launch the code in Listing 7.18 and you will see the following output:

```
Inside simpleMethod in MyAnnotation
Inside simpleMethod in MyAnnotation
```

SUMMARY

This chapter started with a quick overview of Java streams and some stream-oriented classes. You learned about some of the interfaces and classes that support buffered operations, followed by examples of captured user input from the command line using stream-oriented code.

Then you saw how to read the contents of text files, tokenize the lines of text into words, and how to write data to a text file. Then you saw how to serialize and deserialize a custom class, as well as how to count the number of occurrences of a string in a file.

CHAPTER 8

JAVA AND SQL

This chapter contains code samples that illustrate how to access data in MySQL tables from Java. The previous chapter contains code samples that showed you how to work with streams in Java, which is helpful for some of the material in this chapter.

The first part of this chapter briefly introduces SQL (Structured Query Language) and explains major types of SQL statements: DCL, DDL, and DML. The second part of this chapter introduces you to the MySQL database, and shows you various ways of creating and dropping database tables.

The second part of this chapter contains an assortment of SQL statements that contain the SELECT keyword. The third part of this chapter shows you how to write code for connecting with MySQL, how to drop and recreate a MySQL table, and how to select data from a MySQL table.

Note: Remember to set the environment variable CLASSPATH as described later in this chapter for the Java classes that access a MySQL database.

WHAT IS SQL?

SQL is an initialism for Structured Query Language, which is used for managing data in tables in a relational database (RDBMS). SQL commands can be classified in the following four categories:

- DCL (Data Control Language)
- DDL (Data Definition Language)
- DQL (Data Query Language)
- DML (Data Manipulation Language)

The following subsections provide additional information for each item in the preceding list.

What is DCL?

DCL is an acronym for Data Control Language, which refers to any SQL statement that contains the keywords GRANT or REVOKE. These keywords grant or revoke access permissions, respectively, from any database user.

For example, the following SQL statement *grants* (gives) user ABC permission to view and modify records in the employee table:

```
GRANT ALL ON employee
TO ABC;
[WITH GRANT OPTION]
```

The GRANT OPTION enables a user to grant privileges to other database users.

By contrast, the following SQL statement *revokes* (removes) UPDATE privileges on the employee table from user ABC:

```
REVOKE UPDATE
ON employee
FROM ABC;
```

What is DDL?

DDL is an acronym for Data Definition Language, which refers to any SQL statements that contain the following keywords:

- CREATE
- ALTER
- DROP
- RENAME
- TRUNCATE
- COMMENT

The preceding list of keywords can appear in SQL statements that refer to tables as well as views (discussed later). Here are partial examples of the way to use the keywords in the preceding list:

```
ALTER TABLE
CREATE/DROP/TRUNCATE tables
CREATE TABLE abc as (SELECT * from def);
CREATE/DROP/TRUNCATE views
CREATE/DROP indexes
```

DELETE vs. DROP vs. TRUNCATE

These keywords have important differences. The DELETE keyword and the TRUNCATE keyword both delete data from a table, but there can be a significant performance difference. Consider the following SQL statements (the first two delete all the rows from the customers table):

```
DELETE * FROM customers;
TRUNCATE customers;
DROP TABLE customers;
```

The DELETE statement sequentially processes all the rows in the cus-tomers table, whereas the TRUNCATE statement performs one operation to remove all rows from the customers table. Hence, TRUNCATE can be much faster than DELETE when a table contains a large number of rows. By contrast, the DROP statement eliminates the rows *and* the customers table.

Of course, if you want to remove a subset of the rows of the customers table, then you must specify a WHERE clause, so the required SQL statement would be something similar to this statement:

```
DELETE *
FROM customers;
WHERE cust_id < 10000;
```

What is DQL?

DQL is an acronym for Data Query Language, which refers to any SQL statement that contains the keyword SELECT. Note that DQL can involve selecting a subset of data as well as deleting a subset of data, as shown in the following pair of SQL statements:

```
SELECT *
FROM customers
WHERE cust_id < 10000;

DELETE *
FROM customers
WHERE cust_id IN
    (SELECT cust_id FROM customers
     WHERE cust_id < 10000);
```

Although both of the preceding statements have the same effect, the first one is more efficient than the second one, which is also called a *correlated subquery* because the same table is referenced in the outer SQL query and the inner SQL query.

What is DML?

DML is an acronym for Data Manipulation Language, which refers to SQL statements that execute queries against one or more tables in a data-base. DML statements are SQL statements that contain any of the following keywords:

- INSERT
- UPDATE
- DELETE
- MERGE
- CALL
- EXPLAIN PLAN
- LOCK TABLE

In most cases, the preceding keywords modify the existing values of data in one or more tables. For example, the following SQL statement specifies the `INSERT` keyword to insert a new row into the `user` table (the `user` table is defined later in this chapter):

```
INSERT INTO user VALUES (1000, 'Developer');
```

The following SQL statement contains an example of the `UPDATE` keyword to update an attribute of a row:

- `UPDATE user`
- `SET TITLE = 'Team Lead'`
- `WHERE USER_ID = 1000;`

The following SQL query can affect multiple rows in the `TAX_INFO` table:

```
UPDATE tax_info
SET tax_rate = tax_rate + 0.05;
```

What is TCL?

TCL is an acronym for Transaction Control Language, which refers to SQL statements that contain any of the following keywords:

- `COMMIT`
- `ROLLBACK`
- `SAVEPOINT`
- `SET TRANSACTION`

The `COMMIT` keyword commits the results of a SQL statement or a transaction to the underlying database, whereas the `ROLLBACK` keyword serves the opposite purpose. The `SAVEPOINT` keyword identifies a point at which a subsequent transaction can be rolled back, which occurs when the `ROLLBACK` keyword appears in a SQL statement that is executed. The `SET TRANSACTION` statement is used to specify various characteristics of the current transaction, such as the start of a transaction. When the transaction is completed, either the `COMMIT` keyword or the `ROLLBACK` keyword is invoked.

WORKING WITH MYSQL

Oracle provides the MySQL database, which you can download for your operating system:

https://dev.mysql.com/downloads/

Download the MySQL distribution for your machine and perform the installation procedure.

Logging into MySQL

You can log into MySQL as `root` with the following command, which will prompt you for the root password:

```
$ mysql -u root -p
```

If you installed MySQL via a DMG file, then when you launch the preceding command, you will be prompted for the password for the `root` user, which is the same as the password for logging into your laptop.

Creating a MySQL Database

Log into MySQL and invoke the following command to create the `mytools` database:

```
MySQL [mysql]> create database mytools;
Query OK, 1 row affected (0.004 sec)
```

Now select the `mytools` database with the following command:

```
MySQL [mysql]> use mytools;
Database changed
```

Display the tables in the `mytools` database with the following command:

```
MySQL [mytools]> show tables;
Empty set (0.001 sec)
```

The preceding output makes sense because the `mytools` database is an empty database.

CREATING AND DROPPING TABLES

There are three ways to create database tables in MySQL, as well as other RDBMSes. One technique is manual (shown in the next section); another technique (shown second) invokes a SQL file that contains suitable SQL commands; and a third technique involves redirecting a SQL file to the MySQL executable from the command line.

The next section shows you how to create four tables in MySQL using a manual technique that involves explicitly defining a SQL statement from the MySQL prompt and then executing that SQL statement.

Manually Creating MySQL Tables

This section shows how to manually create MySQL tables that are referenced later in this chapter. Specifically, you will see how to create the following tables:

- `customers`
- `friends`
- `weather`

Log into MySQL, and after selecting the `mytools` database, invoke the SQL files in Listing 8.1, Listing 8.2, and Listing 8.3 to create and populate the tables `customers`, `weather`, and `friends`, respectively.

Listing 8.1 displays the content of `customers.sql` that defines the structure of the `customers` table and populates the table with data.

LISTING 8.1: customers.sql

```
DROP TABLE IF EXISTS customers;

CREATE TABLE customers (cust_id INTEGER, first_name
VARCHAR(20), last_name VARCHAR(20), home_address
VARCHAR(20), city VARCHAR(20), state VARCHAR(20), zip_code
VARCHAR(10));

INSERT INTO customers
VALUES (1000,'John','Smith','123 Main
St','Fremont','CA','94123');

INSERT INTO customers
VALUES (2000,'Jane','Jones','123 Main
St','Fremont','CA','95015');
```

Listing 8.2 displays the content of `weather.sql` that defines the structure of the `weather` table and populates the table with data.

LISTING 8.2: weather.sql

```
DROP TABLE IF EXISTS weather;

CREATE TABLE weather (day DATE, temper INTEGER, wind INTEGER, forecast
CHAR(20), city CHAR(20), state CHAR(20));

INSERT INTO weather VALUES('2021-04-01',42, 16,  'Rain', 'sf',  'ca');
INSERT INTO weather VALUES('2021-04-02',45, 3,   'Sunny','sf',  'ca');
INSERT INTO weather VALUES('2021-04-03',78, -12, NULL,   'se',  'wa');
INSERT INTO weather VALUES('2021-07-01',42, 16,  'Rain', '',    'ca');
INSERT INTO weather VALUES('2021-07-02',45, -3,  'Sunny','sf',  'ca');
INSERT INTO weather VALUES('2021-07-03',78, 12,  NULL,   'sf',  'mn');
INSERT INTO weather VALUES('2021-08-04',50, 12,  'Snow', '',    'mn');
INSERT INTO weather VALUES('2021-08-06',51, 32,  '',     'sf',  'ca');
INSERT INTO weather VALUES('2021-09-01',42, 16,  'Rain', 'sf',  'ca');
INSERT INTO weather VALUES('2021-09-02',45, 99,  '',     'sf',  'ca');
INSERT INTO weather VALUES('2021-09-03',15, 12,  'Snow', 'chi', 'il');
```

Listing 8.3 displays the content of `people.sql` that defines the structure of the `people` table and populates the table with data.

LISTING 8.3: people.sql

```
DROP TABLE IF EXISTS people;

CREATE TABLE people (fname varchar(20), lname varchar(20), age
varchar(20), gender char(1), country varchar(20));
```

```
INSERT INTO people VALUES ('john','smith','30','m','usa');

INSERT INTO people VALUES ('jane','smith','31','f','france');
INSERT INTO people VALUES ('jack','jones','32','m','france');
INSERT INTO people VALUES ('dave','stone','33','m','italy');
INSERT INTO people VALUES ('sara','stein','34','f','germany');
INSERT INTO people VALUES ('eddy','bower','35','m','spain');
```

WORKING WITH SIMPLE SELECT STATEMENTS

Earlier in this chapter, you saw examples of the SELECT keyword in SQL statements, and this section contains SQL statements to show you additional ways to select subsets of data from a table. In its simplest form, a SQL statement with the SELECT keyword looks like this:

```
SELECT [one-or-more-attributes]
FROM [one-or-more-tables]
```

Include an asterisk (*) after the SELECT statement if you want to select all the attributes of a table. For example, the following SQL statement illustrates how to select all rows from the people table:

```
MySQL [mytools]> select * from people;
+-------+-------+------+--------+---------+
| fname | lname | age  | gender | country |
+-------+-------+------+--------+---------+
| john  | smith | 30   | m      | usa     |
| jane  | smith | 31   | f      | france  |
| jack  | jones | 32   | m      | france  |
| dave  | stone | 33   | m      | italy   |
| sara  | stein | 34   | f      | germany |
| eddy  | bower | 35   | m      | spain   |
+-------+-------+------+--------+---------+
6 rows in set (0.000 sec)
```

Issue the following SQL statement that contains the LIMIT keyword if you want only the first row from the people table:

```
select * from people limit 1;
+-------+-------+------+--------+---------+
| fname | lname | age  | gender | country |
+-------+-------+------+--------+---------+
| john  | smith | 30   | m      | usa     |
+-------+-------+------+--------+---------+
1 row in set (0.000 sec)
```

Replace the number 1 in the previous SQL query with any other positive integer to display the number of rows that you need. Incidentally, if you replace the number 1 with the number 0, you will see 0 rows returned.

Include the WHERE keyword to specify a condition on the rows, which will return a (possibly empty) subset of rows:

```
SELECT [one-or-more-attributes]
FROM [one-or-more-tables]
WHERE [some condition]
```

For example, the following SQL statement illustrates how to display all the attributes of the rows in the `people` table where the first name is john:

```
MySQL [mytools]> select * from people where fname = 'john';
+-------+-------+------+--------+---------+
| fname | lname | age  | gender | country |
+-------+-------+------+--------+---------+
| john  | smith | 30   | m      | usa     |
+-------+-------+------+--------+---------+
1 row in set (0.000 sec)
```

Include the ORDER BY to specify the order in which you want to display the rows:

```
SELECT *
FROM weather
ORDER BY city;
+------------+--------+------+----------+------+-------+
| day        | temper | wind | forecast | city | state |
+------------+--------+------+----------+------+-------+
| 2021-07-01 |     42 |   16 | Rain     |      | ca    |
| 2021-08-04 |     50 |   12 | Snow     |      | mn    |
| 2021-09-03 |     15 |   12 | Snow     | chi  | il    |
| 2021-04-03 |     78 |  -12 | NULL     | se   | wa    |
| 2021-04-01 |     42 |   16 | Rain     | sf   | ca    |
| 2021-04-02 |     45 |    3 | Sunny    | sf   | ca    |
| 2021-07-02 |     45 |   -3 | Sunny    | sf   | ca    |
| 2021-07-03 |     78 |   12 | NULL     | sf   | mn    |
| 2021-08-06 |     51 |   32 |          | sf   | ca    |
| 2021-09-01 |     42 |   16 | Rain     | sf   | ca    |
| 2021-09-02 |     45 |   99 |          | sf   | ca    |
+------------+--------+------+----------+------+-------+
11 rows in set (0.003 sec)
```

SQL supports a JOIN keyword to retrieve data from two tables that have a common column, as well as GROUP BY and HAVING in SQL statements that group together related items and satisfy additional logical conditions.

The EXISTS Keyword

The EXISTS keyword selects a row based on the existence of a value.

```
select city, state
from weather where exists
(select city from weather where city = 'abc');
Empty set (0.001 sec)
```

The preceding is somewhat contrived because it can be replaced with this simpler and intuitive query:

```
select city, state
from weather
where city = 'abc';
```

The LIMIT Keyword

The `LIMIT` keyword limits the number of rows that are in a result set. For example, the `weather` table contains 11 rows, as shown here:

```
SELECT COUNT(*) FROM weather;
+----------+
| count(*) |
+----------+
|       11 |
+----------+
1 row in set (0.001 sec)
```

If we want to see only three rows instead of all the rows in the `weather` table, issue the following SQL query:

```
SELECT city,state
FROM weather ORDER
BY state, city
LIMIT 3;
+------+-------+
| city | state |
+------+-------+
|      | ca    |
| sf   | ca    |
| sf   | ca    |
+------+-------+
3 rows in set (0.000 sec)
```

DELETE, TRUNCATE, AND DROP IN SQL

SQL enables you to delete *all* the data from a table in several ways. One way is to invoke the following SQL statement:

```
DELETE * from customers;
```

However, if a database table has a large number of rows, a faster technique is the `TRUNCATE` statement, as shown here:

```
TRUNCATE customers;
```

Both of the preceding commands involve removing rows from a table without dropping the table. If you want to drop the rows in a table *and* the table as well, use the `DROP` statement as shown here:

```
DROP TABLE IF EXISTS customers;
```

More Options for the DELETE Statement in SQL

The preceding section showed you how to delete all the rows in a table, and this section shows you how to delete a subset of the rows in a table, which involves specifying a condition for the rows that you want to drop from a table.

The following SQL statement deletes the rows in the `customers` table where the first name is JOHN:

```
DELETE
FROM customers
Where FNAME = 'JOHN';
```

The next SQL statement deletes the rows in the customers table where the first name is JOHN and the rows in the `purchase_orders` table that are associated with JOHN:

```
DELETE
FROM customers
Where FNAME = 'JOHN'
CASCADE;
```

The preceding statement is called a *cascading delete*, and it is very useful when the rows in a table have external dependencies. For example, the `customers` table has a one-to-many relationship with the `purchase_orders` table; hence, if you remove a "parent" row from the `customers` table, you want to remove the "child" rows from the `purchase_orders` table.

You can also specify the `LIMIT` keyword with `DELETE`, an example of which is shown here:

```
DELETE
FROM customers
Where FNAME = 'JOHN'
LIMIT 1;
```

The preceding statement will delete one row, but there is an exception: the preceding SQL query will delete all rows whose name equals JOHN if you specify ON DELETE CASCADE in the table definition of the `customers` table.

WHAT IS A SQL INDEX?

An *index* is a construct that enables the faster retrieval of records from database tables and therefore improves performance. An index contains an entry that corresponds to each row in a table, and the index itself is stored in a tree-like structure. SQL enables you to define one or more indexes for a table, and some guidelines are provided in a subsequent section.

By way of analogy, the index of a book enables you to search for a word or a term and locate the associated page number(s) so you can then navigate to one of those pages. Clearly, the use of the book index is much faster than looking sequentially through every page in the book.

Types of Indexes

A *unique index* prevents duplicate values in a column, provided that the column is also uniquely indexed, which can be performed automatically if a table has a primary key.

A *clustered index* changes the order of the rows in a table, and then performs a search that is based in the key values. A table can have only one clustered index.

MySQL 8 introduced *invisible indexes* that are unavailable for the query optimizer. MySQL ensures that those indexes are kept current when data in the referenced column are modified. You can make indexes invisible by explicitly declare their visibility during table creation or via the ALTER TABLE command, which is not discussed in this chapter.

Creating an Index

An index on a MySQL table can be defined in two convenient ways:

• As part of the table definition during table creation
• After the table has been created

Here is an example of creating an index on the full_name attribute *during* the creation of the table friend_table:

```
DROP TABLE IF EXISTS friend_table;

CREATE TABLE friend_table  (
   friend_id int(8) NOT NULL AUTO_INCREMENT,
   full_name varchar(40) NOT NULL,
   fname varchar(20) NOT NULL,
   lname varchar(20) NOT NULL,
   PRIMARY KEY (friend_id), INDEX(full_name)
);
```

Here is an example of creating index friend_lname_idx on the lname attribute *after* the creation of the table friend_table:

```
CREATE INDEX friend_lname_idx ON friend_table(lname);
Query OK, 0 rows affected (0.035 sec)
Records: 0  Duplicates: 0  Warnings: 0
```

You can create an index on multiple columns, an example of which is shown here:

```
CREATE INDEX friend_lname_fname_idx ON friend_
table(lname,fname);
```

An index on a MySQL table can specify a maximum of 16 indexed columns.

Overhead of Indexes

An index occupies some memory on secondary storage. In general, if you issue a SQL statement that involves an index, that index is first loaded into memory and then it's utilized to access the appropriate record(s). A SQL query that involves simply accessing (reading) data via an index is almost always more efficient than accessing data without an index.

However, if a SQL statement *updates* records in one or more tables, then *all* the affected indexes must be updated. As a result, there can be a performance impact when multiple indexes are updated as a result of updating table data. Hence, it's important to determine a suitable number of indexes, and the columns in each of those indexes, which can be done either by experimentation (not recommended for beginners) or via SQL tools (some are open source and others are commercial) that provide statistics regarding the performance of SQL statements when indexes are involved.

Considerations for Defining Indexes

A full table scan for large tables will likely be computationally expensive, so make sure that you define indexes on columns that are referenced in the WHERE clause in your SQL statements. As a simple example, consider the following SQL statement:

```
SELECT *
FROM customers
WHERE lname = 'Smith';
```

If you do not have an index that includes the lname *attribute of the* customers *table, then a full table scan is executed.*

Consider defining an index on attributes that appear in query statements that involve SELECT, GROUP BY, ORDER BY, or JOIN. As mentioned earlier, updates to table data necessitate updates to indexes, which in turn can result in lower performance.

A suggestion before inserting a large volume of data into a table (or tables):

1. Disable the indexes.
2. Insert the data.
3. Enable the indexes again.

Although the preceding approach involves rebuilding the indexes, which is performed after Step 3, you might see a performance improvement compared to directly inserting the table data. Of course, you could also try both approaches and calculate the time required to complete the data insertion.

As yet another option, it's possible to perform a multi-row insert in MySQL, which enables you to insert several rows with a single SQL statement, thereby reducing the number of times the indexes must be updated. The maximum number of rows that can be inserted via a multi-row insert depends on the value of max_allowed_packet (whose default value is 4M), as described here:

https://dev.mysql.com/doc/refman/5.7/en/packet-too-large.html

Another suggestion: check the order of the columns in multi-column indexes and compare that order with the order of the columns in each index. *MySQL will only use an index if the left-leading column is referenced.*

CONNECTING TO MYSQL IN JAVA

There are two steps that you need to perform before you can compile and launch the Java code in this section.

The first step involves downloading a JAR file for the database operations, which you can download from this website:

https://dev.mysql.com/downloads/connector/j/

The second step involves updating the CLASSPATH environment variable to include the JAR file that you downloaded in the previous step (the actual version number might be different):

```
export CLASSPATH=$CLASSPATH:.:mysql-connector-java-8.0.18.
jar:
```

Listing 8.4 displays the content of MySQLCONNECT.java that illustrates how to connect to a MySQL database.

LISTING 8.4: MySQLCONNECT.java

```java
import java.sql.Connection;
import java.sql.DriverManager;
import java.sql.ResultSet;
import java.sql.Statement;

class MySQLCONNECT
{
    public static void main(String args[])
    {
        try {
          //deprecated class:
          //Class.forName("com.mysql.jdbc.Driver");
            Class.forName("com.mysql.cj.jdbc.Driver");

            // mytools/root/yourpassword = database/username/
            password
            Connection conn = DriverManager.getConnection(
                "jdbc:mysql://127.0.0.1:3306/
                mytools?serverTimezone=UTC",
                "root", "yourpassword");

            conn.close();
            System.out.println("Successfully connected to
            MySQL");
        } catch(Exception e){
            System.out.println("Something is wrong");
            System.out.println(e);
            // Something is wrong:
            // java.lang.ClassNotFoundException: com.mysql.
            cj.jdbc.Driver
            // export CLASSPATH=mysql-connector-java-8.0.18.
            jar:$CLASSPATH
        }
```

```
        finally { }
    }
}

/*
java.sql.SQLException: The server time zone value 'PDT'
is unrecognized or represents more than one time zone.
You must configure either the server or JDBC driver (via
the serverTimezone configuration property) to use a more
specific time zone value if you want to utilize time zone
support.
*/
```

Listing 8.4 starts with several import statements that specify Java classes that are located in the JDBC JAR file, which is also included in the CLASSPATH environment variable (otherwise, the code will not compile successfully).

The next section of code initializes the string variables URL, USER, and PASS. If need be, replace mytools with your own database (either an existing database or a new database) and also specify the correct value for PASS.

The next portion of Listing 8.4 is the main() method that contains a try/catch block in which a database connection is established. If an error occurs, then the catch() block displays a stack trace that describes the error that was encountered. Launch the code in Listing 8.4 and you will see the following output:

```
Successfully connected to MySQL
```

DROP AND RECREATE A MYSQL TABLE

Make sure that you perform the two steps in the previous section before you compile and launch the code in this section. Listing 8.5 displays the content of the Java class MySQLDROPTABLE.java that illustrates how to connect to a MySQL database and drop and recreate a table.

LISTING 8.5: MySQLDROPTABLE.java

```
import java.sql.Connection;
import java.sql.DriverManager;
import java.sql.ResultSet;
import java.sql.Statement;

class MySQLDROPTABLE
{
    public static void main(String args[])
    {
      try {
        //deprecated class:
        //Class.forName("com.mysql.jdbc.Driver");
          Class.forName("com.mysql.cj.jdbc.Driver");
```

```
// mytools/root/yourpassword = database/username/
password
Connection conn = DriverManager.getConnection(
        "jdbc:mysql://127.0.0.1:3306/
        mytools?serverTimezone=UTC",
        "root","yourpassword");
        //"jdbc:mysql://localhost:3306/mytools",
        //"root","yourpassword");

// employees table: emp_id, mgr_id, title
Statement stmt = conn.createStatement();
stmt.executeUpdate("DROP TABLE IF EXISTS
EMPLOYEES");

String sql = "CREATE TABLE employees " +
            "(emp_id INT(8), "+
            " mgr_id INT(8), " +
            " title VARCHAR(200), " +
            " PRIMARY KEY ( emp_id ))";

    stmt.executeUpdate(sql);
    conn.close();
} catch(Exception e){
    System.out.println(e);
}
finally { }
}
}
```

Listing 8.5 starts with several `import` statements that specify Java classes that are located in the JDBC JAR file, which is also included in the CLASSPATH environment variable (otherwise, the code will not compile successfully).

The next section of code initializes the string variables URL, USER, and PASS. You must replace `mytools` with your own database (either an existing database or a new database) and also specify the correct value for PASS.

The next portion of Listing 8.5 is the `main()` method that contains a `try/catch` block in which a database connection is established, and the string variable `sql1` is initialized to a SQL statement for dropping the `friends` table if it already exists. The third step initializes the string variable `sql2` with a SQL statement for creating the `friends` table.

The fourth step executes the SQL code in the string variables `sql1` and `sql2`. If an error occurs, then the `catch()` block displays a stack trace that describes the error that was encountered. Launch the code in Listing 8.5 and you will see the following output:

```
Created table FRIENDS in database
```

Note that older versions of code in the JDBC JAR file require explicitly closing the database connection, whereas this step is now performed automatically.

Launch the code in Listing 8.5 and you will not see any output. However, you can log into MySQL and execute the following SQL statements to verify that the `employees` table does exist:

```
MySQL [mytools]> desc employees;
+---------+--------------+------+-----+---------+-------+
| Field   | Type         | Null | Key | Default | Extra |
+---------+--------------+------+-----+---------+-------+
| emp_id  | int          | NO   | PRI | NULL    |       |
| mgr_id  | int          | YES  |     | NULL    |       |
| title   | varchar(200) | YES  |     | NULL    |       |
+---------+--------------+------+-----+---------+-------+
3 rows in set (0.001 sec)

MySQL [mytools]> select * from employees;
Empty set (0.001 sec)
```

INSERT DATA INTO A MYSQL TABLE

Listing 8.6 displays the content of `MySQLINSERT.java` that illustrates how to insert data into a database table.

LISTING 8.6: MySQLINSERT.java

```java
import java.sql.Connection;
import java.sql.DriverManager;
import java.sql.ResultSet;
import java.sql.Statement;

class MySQLINSERT
{
   public static void main(String args[])
   {
      try {
        //deprecated class:
        //Class.forName("com.mysql.jdbc.Driver");
          Class.forName("com.mysql.cj.jdbc.Driver");

          // mytools/root/yourpassword = database/username/
          password
          Connection conn = DriverManager.getConnection(
                "jdbc:mysql://127.0.0.1:3306/
                mytools?serverTimezone=UTC",
                "root","yourpassword");
                //"jdbc:mysql://localhost:3306/mytools",
                //"root","yourpassword");

          // employees table: emp_id, mgr_id, title
          Statement stmt = conn.createStatement();
          stmt.executeUpdate("DROP TABLE IF EXISTS
          EMPLOYEES");

          // recreate the employees table:
```

```
String sql = "CREATE TABLE employees " +
             "(emp_id INT(8), "+
             " mgr_id INT(8), " +
             " title VARCHAR(200), " +
             " PRIMARY KEY ( emp_id ))";
stmt.executeUpdate(sql);

// insert data into employees table:
String sql1;
sql1 = "INSERT INTO employees VALUES (1000, 2000,
'Developer');";
stmt.executeUpdate(sql1);

sql1 = "INSERT INTO employees VALUES (2000, 3000,
'Project Lead');";
stmt.executeUpdate(sql1);

sql1 = "INSERT INTO employees VALUES (3000, 4000,
'Dev Manager');";
stmt.executeUpdate(sql1);

sql1 = "INSERT INTO employees VALUES (4000, 4000,
'Senior Dev Manager');";
stmt.executeUpdate(sql1);

      conn.close();
    } catch(Exception e){
      System.out.println(e);
    }
    finally { }
  }
}
```

Listing 8.6 starts with several `import` statements that specify Java classes that are located in the JDBC JAR file, which is also included in the CLASSPATH environment variable (otherwise, the code will not compile successfully).

The next section of code initializes the string variables URL, USER, and PASS. You must replace `mytools` with your own database (either an existing database or a new database) and also specify the correct value for PASS.

The next portion of Listing 8.6 is the `main()` method that contains a try/ catch block in which a database connection is established, and the string variable `del1` is initialized to a SQL statement for deleting the rows in the `friends` table. The next step initializes the string variable `sql` with a SQL statement for inserting a row of data into the `friends` table. This step is executed twice more with different data values.

Launch the code in Listing 8.6 and you will not see any output. However, you can log into MySQL and execute the following SQL statements to verify that the `employees` table does exist and contains data:

```
MySQL [mytools]> desc employees;
+---------+--------------+------+-----+---------+-------+
| Field   | Type         | Null | Key | Default | Extra |
+---------+--------------+------+-----+---------+-------+
| emp_id  | int          | NO   | PRI | NULL    |       |
| mgr_id  | int          | YES  |     | NULL    |       |
| title   | varchar(200) | YES  |     | NULL    |       |
+---------+--------------+------+-----+---------+-------+
3 rows in set (0.001 sec)

MySQL [mytools]> select * from employees;
+--------+--------+--------------------+
| emp_id | mgr_id | title              |
+--------+--------+--------------------+
|   1000 |   2000 | Developer          |
|   2000 |   3000 | Project Lead       |
|   3000 |   4000 | Dev Manager        |
|   4000 |   4000 | Senior Dev Manager |
+--------+--------+--------------------+
4 rows in set (0.000 sec)
```

SELECT DATA FROM A MYSQL TABLE

Listing 8.7 displays the content of MySQLSELECT.java that illustrates how to select data from a database table.

LISTING 8.7: MySQLSELECT.java

```java
import java.sql.Connection;

import java.sql.Connection;
import java.sql.DriverManager;
import java.sql.ResultSet;
import java.sql.Statement;

class MySQLSELECT
{
   public static void main(String args[])
{
   int rowCount = 0;

   try {
      Class.forName("com.mysql.cj.jdbc.Driver");

      Connection conn = DriverManager.getConnection(
          "jdbc:mysql://127.0.0.1:3306/mytools?serverTimez
one=UTC","username","password");

      // employees table: emp_id, mgr_id, title
      Statement stmt = conn.createStatement();
      ResultSet rs = stmt.executeQuery("SELECT * FROM
EMPLOYEES");

      // display the contents of the EMPLOYEES table:
      while(rs.next())
```

```
    {
      System.out.println(rs.getInt(1)+" "+rs.
      getString(2)+" "+rs.getString(3));
      ++rowCount;
    }
    conn.close();
  } catch(Exception e){
    System.out.println(e);
  }
  finally {
    System.out.println("Row Count = "+rowCount);
  }
}
```

Listing 8.7 starts with several `import` statements that specify Java classes that are located in the JDBC JAR file, which is also included in the CLASSPATH environment variable (otherwise, the code will not compile successfully).

The next section of code initializes the string variables URL, USER, and PASS. You must replace `mytools` with your own database (either an existing database or a new database) and also specify the correct value for PASS.

The next portion of Listing 8.7 is the `main()` method that contains a `try/catch` block in which a database connection is established, and the string variable `del1` is initialized to a SQL statement for deleting the rows in the friends table. The next step initializes the string variable `sql` with a SQL statement for inserting a row of data into the `employees` table. This step is executed twice more with different data values. Launch the code in Listing 8.7 and you will see the following output:

```
first and lastname: Jane Jones
first and lastname: John Smith
first and lastname: Sally Stone
first and lastname: Dave Edwards
```

NEXT STEPS

Now that you have an understanding of basic concepts in Java, there are other interesting aspects of Java that you can learn, which are listed here in three groups.

Java Threads and Sockets

- Basic Thread Concepts
- Extending the Java Thread Class
- Implementing the Java Runnable Interface
- Sharing Data Among Java Threads
- Working with a Java `ThreadGroup`
- Thread-related Exceptions
- Executing Multiple Java Threads

- A Simple Race Condition in Java Threads
- Java Synchronization
- Java Threads in a Deadlocked State

Java Networking

- The `URLConnection` Class
- Making an HTTP `GET` Request
- Making an HTTP `POST` Request
- Working with HTTP/2
- A Server-Side Socket
- A Secure Server-Side Socket
- A Client-Side Socket Example
- Sending JSON Data from a Server Socket
- Client Socket Requests for JSON Data
- Sending JSON Data from a Server Socket

Reflection, GC, and Classloaders

- Launching a Process inside Java
- Java Reflection
- Java System-Related Commands
- Garbage Collection
- Invoking `System.exit()`
- Java `ClassLoaders`
- Types of Java `ClassLoaders`
- `java.lang.ClassLoader` Methods

SUMMARY

In this chapter, you were introduced to SQL (Structured Query Language) and major types of SQL statements, such as DCL, DDL, and DML. Then you saw how to execute various SQL commands from MySQL, such as creating a MySQL database. You also learned how to create database tables and how to populate them with data.

In addition, you saw an assortment of SQL statements that contain the `SELECT` keyword.

Next, you learned how to connect to a MySQL database using Java code. Furthermore, you saw how to create a database table, populate the table with data, and then retrieve data from that table. Finally, you learned how to read `JSON`-based data in Java.

Congratulations! You have successfully completed a fast-paced introductory Java book with a plethora of concepts and code samples that provides you with a foundation from which you can learn more advanced concepts. Good luck on your journey!

INDEX